Historic Churches of the South

Historic Churches

of the South

A Collection of Articles Published in

Holland's

THE MAGAZINE OF THE SOUTH

Selected and edited by

MARY LORRAINE SMITH

Associate Editor of Holland's Magazine

TUPPER & LOVE, INC.

ATLANTA

PHOTOGRAPHS on pages 2, 4, 5, 8, 99 — Thurston
Hatcher and courtesy of Virginia State Chamber
of Commerce: 10 — Louis C. Williams: 24 — C.
C. Springfield: 32, 93, 45 — John E. Thierman:
36 — by courtesy of New Orleans Association of
Commerce: 40 — Ann Moreton: 60 — John Blun-
dell: 64 — John Lipscomb: 68 — H. L. Sommer-
ville: 69 — Elicson: 74 — Robert H. Walston:
81 — Slade of Tallahassee: 86 — Knabb Lane
Studio: 89 — Foltz: 90 — Virgil F. Greenlee:
102 — George Schaeffer: 107 — Earl Tye: 111 —
Richard Garrison: 115 — Ronald Allen Reilly.

Printed and bound

in the United States of America

FOOTE & DAVIES, INC.

Atlanta, Georgia

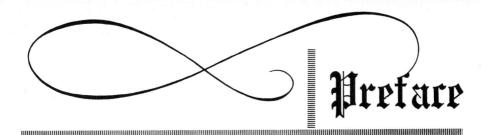

Preface

THE VENERABLE old churches which dot the South are among the region's most interesting historic landmarks. Their story is the story of the religious groups that have ministered to the spiritual—and often to the temporal—needs of the South throughout Colonial and pioneer days, the destructive years of the War Between the States, the trials of the Reconstruction period, and the later years of rapid economic and industrial development.

Each of these churches has played an important part in the building of the South, whether it is a cathedral, rich in art treasures, or a simple frame meeting house in a rural community; a church that is actively serving the needs of a large city congregation, or a small country church kept alive only by the determined efforts of a few faithful members.

Since it would be impossible to tell the story of all the Southern churches of note in one small volume, a number of famous houses of worship have, of necessity, been omitted. The churches whose story is told here were selected because they are denominationally and geographically representative, as well as historically significant.

MARY LORRAINE SMITH

Contents

Historic Churches of the South

Historic Churches of the South

The tower of Jamestown Church still stands on its island in the James River, a monument to the first permanent English settlement in America.

A BELL
A STEEPLE   VIRGINIA
AN OPEN DOOR

LIBERTY WAS CRADLED in the churches of Colonial Virginia, and theirs is the story of a determined people who valued above life itself the right to worship in the church of their choice. Many of these historic churches still stand, symbols of the religious freedom that has become one of the basic tenets of our American way of life.

On April 13, 1952, the somber tones of the bell in the high octagonal steeple of Bruton Parish Church in Williamsburg called members and visitors to the 237th Easter Service to be held within its walls.

High above its green setting the old steeple beckons you on down Duke of Gloucester Street to the ivy-covered brick church. In the walled churchyard are the graves of two royal governors of Virginia, councilors, attorneys, teachers, and numerous other important figures of colonial days.

But the story of this church begins in another place. On April 26, 1607, a group of 105 Englishmen sighted land in Chesapeake Bay, and a few of them rowed ashore to erect a wooden cross commemorating their safe arrival in the New World.

They continued their voyage up a wide river which they named the James. On May 13, 1607, their three small ships—the "Sarah Constant," the "Goodspeed," and the "Discovery"—were "moored to trees in six fathoms of water." Early the next day these men started building James Towne, the first permanent English settlement in America.

3 ...

Completed in 1715, Bruton Parish Church in Williamsburg is perhaps the oldest church building in continuous use in Virginia. Its beautifully simple lines are typical of the best in colonial church architecture.

Historic Churches of the South

At first the Reverend Robert Hunt held church services under a canvas stretched across the branches of trees. Then, in 1609, the settlers completed a log church building. It became their refuge and the center of life in the community.

During the first years there was need for refuge, for disaster seemed to stalk the community. Heat, famine, illness, Indian attacks and death trod upon each other's heels in discouraging procession. To the church the settlers came for courage, for guidance, and for shelter. Their dead were buried under its floor, and the sick and wounded lay on its benches. In happier times, they gathered there for marriages, christenings, and Sunday services. Eventually good corn and tobacco crops matured, the London Company sent wives for the men, and there were long periods of peace with the Indians.

...4

Sir George Yeardley and his wife, Temperance Flowerdew, were regular communicants of the Jamestown church during his terms as the London Company's Governor of Virginia. In 1619, he was instructed to establish the House of Burgesses, the first legislative assembly in America. Two men from each "town and hundred and particular plantation" met with him and the council in the Jamestown church. And so it was that this church with its rude wooden benches held the first law-making body in English America.

Jamestown suffered four fires. In one of these the church was completely demolished. It was not replaced until in the 1680's when the James City Parish completed a brick church with a heavy

The interior of Bruton Parish Church looks just as it did over two centuries ago when the royal governors of Virginia attended its services.

Gothic entrance tower. In this chapel they placed their baptismal font and the Communion service which had been given to them by Acting Governor Francis Moryson. The chalice and paten were inscribed:

"MIXE NOT HOLY THINGS WITH PROFANE
EX DONO FRANCISCI MORRISON ARMEGERI ANNO DONO 1661."

Today the ivy-mantled tower of this historic church still stands. It is used as the entrance to the restored church on the island in the James River, and is cared for by the Association for the Preservation of Virginia Antiquities and the National Park Service.

In 1676-77, during Bacon's Rebellion, the statehouse was burned and the General Assembly held its sessions at Middle Plantation. Located some seven miles inland on higher ground, this spot was chosen as the site of the new capital when in 1699 the Assembly voted to leave Jamestown. The new capital was named Williamsburg.

Running through the center of the new capital was Duke of Gloucester Street—a thoroughfare "nine poles wide." It passed directly in front of the little Middle Plantation church and ended at the circular entrance to the College of William and Mary. The vestry of the James City Parish later gave their Communion service to Bruton Parish.

The vestry decided to build a new church for Bruton Parish. Lieutenant-Governor Alexander Spotswood submitted to the vestry a "platt or draught" for the building in 1711, and the new church was completed in 1715. It was built in the form of a Roman cross with a square entrance, a heavy tower, and a beautifully simple interior. It was much like the other colonial churches of this period except that, being the court church, it had a special pew to be used by the royal governor.

This box was placed directly in front of the dark wood pulpit
with its high sounding board, and was draped with a crimson cur-

tain. In his high-backed chair Lieutenant-Governor Spotswood sat through many a service conducted by the man who was known as the governor-breaker and who served for many years as the rector of Bruton Parish. He was the Reverend James Blair, commissary of the Bishop of London and president of the College of William and Mary.

It was quite fashionable to attend the court church. Chaises and coaches swung down Duke of Gloucester Street to bring the ladies from the great houses along the York and the James to service during legislative sessions. Members of the assembly, faculty members from the college, and visiting planters and lawyers paused in the vestibule for whispered conversations before they entered.

Prominent among the early vestrymen were George Wythe, the first professor of law in an American college, and Henry Tyler, great-great grandfather of President Tyler. George Washington's name appears eleven times in the church record. As young men, Thomas Jefferson, Monroe, Tyler, Edmund Randolph, John Marshall and Winfield Scott sat in the west and south galleries, sections reserved for college students.

The church grew so fast that in 1752 it was necessary to make a 25-foot addition to the chancel end; the organ loft was built in 1755 at the time that Braddock and George Washington, resplendent in the King's uniform, were receiving plaudits for their successes in the French and Indian Wars. John Tarpley thought that there should be a bell in the steeple, so he presented one to the vestry in 1761.

That bell became famous as the Liberty Bell of Virginia. On June 1, 1774, it summoned twenty-five members of the House of Burgesses to a day's fasting, humiliation and prayer—the port of Boston had been closed by the Crown, in retaliation for the Boston Tea Party. And from that meeting went out the call for the first Virginia Convention.

Christ's Church in Alexandria, Virginia, is filled with mementos of the days when George and Martha Washington were among its communicants.

The bell pealed forth a jubilant announcement of the repeal of the Stamp Act, and on May 15, 1776, its somber tones heralded the first act of sovereignty by any of the colonies, a full six weeks before the Philadelphia bell proclaimed the message. It boomed forth as the Union Jack was hauled down from the Williamsburg capitol. It heralded the celebration of peace with Great Britain, proclaimed at Williamsburg on May 1, 1783, while the guns sounded and fireworks curved over its steeple.

In 1839-40, the interior of the church was rearranged, the pews were altered, and the graves of some of the important persons were moved from under the stone flags of the floor. The church structure, however, survived the War Between the States and the remodeling fever of the Victorian Era, and entered the Twentieth Century outwardly the same.

In 1905-07 the Reverend W. A. R. Goodwin, rector of the church, began the restoration of the interior. He also began his crusade for the restoration of the city of Williamsburg at about this time. Most of us know the story of how he enlisted the interest and backing of John D. Rockefeller, Jr., and of the progress of this monumental restoration.

Bruton Parish Church has been completely restored. Its door is open on weekdays, and visitors are always welcome at services. It is a hospitable church, this court-church which has witnessed so much history in the making. Inside you may look at the baptismal font which tradition says was used at the baptism of Pocahontas. Two Communion services, the Jamestown and the King George III, are in the church. A third service, willed to the College of William and Mary by Lady Gooch, is to be seen there. The Pulpit Bible was the gift of King Edward VII, and the lectern upon which it rests was presented by President Theodore Roosevelt. The present Prayer Desk Bible was given by President Woodrow Wilson.

As visitors leave the church most of them pause beside one of

It was in the second Virginia Revolutionary Convention in old St. John's in Richmond that Patrick Henry delivered his famous liberty-or-death speech.

the more recent graves. Here lies the Reverend W. A. R. Goodwin. This restored church—in fact the whole Williamsburg Restoration—is his monument. His vision, enthusiasm and hard work made a dream a reality.

St. John's Church in Richmond took its place in history in 1775, when Lord Dunmore, Royal Governor of Virginia, became so hostile to the members of the House of Burgesses that it was necessary for them to seek another meeting place—one further removed from his eyes—for the second Virginia Convention. So they met in Richmond to consider the question of American rights. The isolation by road and by water made the little town a comparatively safe place. So many of the prominent men of the colony had been invited to the meeting that it was necessary to use the largest public building available. It was the church on Richmond Hill. We know it today as St. John's on Church Hill.

Historic Churches of the South

Richmond's leaders must have made some hurried apologies to the men from Williamsburg, accustomed to the palatial comforts of the capital city. This simple frame building in which they met was "60 feet long, 25 feet broad, with a pitch of 14 feet, finished after the moddle of Curl's Church."

It was several days before any important matter was brought before the convention. In the evenings the gentlemen gathered in little cliques to discuss privately the issues under consideration. Prominent in one of these groups was a man from Hanover, a lean fellow with a thin face and a big nose, who advocated arming the Virginia colony. His name was Patrick Henry.

On about the third day, when the convention was considering a resolution thanking the Assembly of Jamaica for its memorial to the King in behalf of the American colonies, and expressing a desire for peace, Patrick Henry leaped to his feet. As soon as the chair recognized him he moved to the end of the pew and began to speak. Men moved forward in their seats, and an electric silence fell over the room, as they listened to the immortal words:

11 . . .

"Gentlemen may cry peace! Peace! . . . but there is no peace. The war is actually begun. The next gale that sweeps from the North will bring to our ears the clash of resounding arms! Our brethren are already in the field . . . Is life so dear, or peace so sweet, as to be purchased at the price of chains and slavery? Forbid it, Almighty God! I know not what course others may take; but as for me, give me liberty or give me death!"

Historians tell us that the effect of this speech was so powerful that Colonel Edward Carrington, listening at a window of the church, cried: "Let me be buried at this spot." When he died in 1810, his wish was respected.

The list of those present on that day included such men as Thomas Jefferson, George Washington, George Mason, George Wythe, Richard Henry Lee, Benjamin Harrison, Peyton Randolph and Archibald Cary.

Today the steeple of St. John's rises in simple dignity through the trees on Church Hill, a beacon to those who seek the open door. The white frame structure is possibly three times as large as it was in 1775. But the pews are the same, the glass windows are there, and the same pulpit and sounding board of dark wood enhance the interior. Edgar Allan Poe's mother rests in the church-yard, as does George Wythe, and about them are others who have lived in and helped to build Richmond.

People in Richmond will tell you that Benedict Arnold used the church as barracks for his soldiers when he occupied the city. And some, who love old books, will let you read George Wythe Munford's *The Two Parsons*. It tells the story of the Reverend John Buchanan, rector of St. John's in the day when the Presbyterians and the Episcopalians shared the state capitol building as a meeting place because the church on the hill was "too far out."

But freedom was not won when the battles of the Revolution were ended. At the close of the Revolutionary War, the fear of

danger passed, and the yearning for liberty passed with it. We had won the war, and our heritage was held lightly by many of the colonists. Apathy was widespread; people did not wish to take the time to vote. From 1781 through 1789, our democracy showed every symptom of failure. George Washington was asked to be king. Then Congress met and sent a call to all the states for delegates to come to the Constitutional Convention. From May 14 to September 17 the delegates from twelve states worked in a lonely effort to formulate the principles on which our nation is founded. It was then that liberty was born.

Some of the men whose experience, wisdom and courage went into this undertaking were from the churches of Virginia—George Mason, George Wythe, Thomas Jefferson and James Madison. And on the way home from Philadelphia they stopped off with George Washington for a conference at Mount Vernon. As the months passed they returned, and sometimes they attended church with Washington in Alexandria. Known as Christ's Church, this little church has since become famous for the number of Presidents of the United States who have attended services there. The sun shines on the silver plate which marks the Washington pew, purchased for the sum of 36 pounds 10 shillings in about 1774. In this same pew, on a Sunday in January 1942, Winston Churchill worshipped with the late President Roosevelt. General Robert E. Lee was confirmed in this church.

The acre of ground on which it was established was given by John Alexander of Stafford. In 1765, George Washington was elected a member of the vestry. From that time until his death he was actively associated with this church.

In 1767, James Parsons was given the contract to build the church but he did not fulfill his agreement and the church was completed by James Carlyle in 1773. In the same year James Wren was authorized to write the Lord's Prayer, the Creed and the Ten Commandments on panels which may be seen today on each side of the pulpit. The organ and the steeple were added to the church building in 1810, and a bell was presented in 1818.

Many people visit these colonial churches each year. Visitors leave with a feeling of reverent awe and thoughtful meditation, for these churches serve as continuing witnesses of the fact that religious freedom is an eternal element in our American way of life.

And throughout our land there are churches with steeples, with bells that mark the hours, and with open doors. Whatever your faith, there is a place you can call your own. This is our gift from those who nurtured liberty, as it was cradled in the colonial churches of Tidewater Virginia.

—LOU HENSLEE

Historic Churches of the South

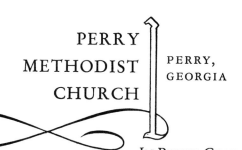

PERRY METHODIST CHURCH

PERRY, GEORGIA

IN PERRY, GEORGIA, there stands a paradox. In this deeply Southern town the Methodist Church is as pure New England in its architecture as if it faced upon the Boston commons. But even more unusual is the story behind it. Built for a congregation of slave owners, its builder was a Negro.

Back in 1850 a wealthy planter, W. M. Davis, lived on the Santee River in South Carolina. He owned hundreds of slaves, and his plantation prospered until a new grass took hold of his land and threatened to ruin his crops. Unable to get rid of the pest, Mr. Davis finally decided to leave South Carolina and move to Georgia.

Among Davis' slaves was one young man named Pete who showed unusual intelligence and an aptitude for building. Mr. Davis told Pete that he would send him to the North to study building and design, if he would come back and build a new home for his master in Georgia. Upon completion of the job, he would be a free man. "Pete, I know you will keep your part of the bargain," Mr. Davis told him as he saw him off.

Mr. Davis moved his family to Houston County, Georgia, where they occupied a small house while they waited for Pete to complete his training. Their new neighbors scoffed. "You've just lost a good slave. You don't really think he'll come back after he has had a taste of freedom." They even made bets on it. Mr. Davis kept quiet but he never lost faith in Pete. And his faith was justified, for Pete kept his promise. When he returned, he built a fine home for his master. His work was so good that the house stands

Historic Churches of the South

15 . . .

Perry Methodist Church was built by a slave in return for his freedom.

today, almost unchanged. It took him seven years to build it and earn his freedom.

Then, just as the Davis home was nearing completion, fire destroyed the Methodist Church in the community. Pete knew his master loved the church, and he told Mr. Davis that he would stay long enough to help build another one. "But, Pete, you're free now," Davis insisted. "That was our bargain. You can go back North and find work." But Pete stayed. Two of Mr. Davis' grandchildren, who live in Perry today, tell the story as their mother told it to them. How Pete went to the forests and selected each tree to be cut, how he labored over the design and construction of the building. The Davis slaves worked with Pete, and in 1861 the church was finished. Shortly afterward Pete left for New York to work for a firm of architects, and the town of Perry heard little more of him. But he left part of himself behind. The little church, so typical of the New England architecture of that day, still stands as a symbol of his loyalty and devotion to the man who gave him his education and his freedom.

During recent years the town of Perry has grown and the church membership has grown with it. During the depression years an addition had to be made to the building, but the results were not altogether satisfactory and some years later the stewards agreed to have an architect design a more appropriate addition. The architect's drawings, in keeping with the style of the original structure, met with the congregation's approval but the construction costs were prohibitive. As the bids came in from various contractors, it began to look as though the building project would have to be dropped.

Many of the stewards were reluctant to abandon the project, and the chairman of the building committee, in particular, felt that the plans must be carried out. He decided to go into the contracting business himself and he built the new addition according to the exacting details of the architect's plan—at actual cost! The congregation raised the necessary funds and the addition was completely free of debt upon its completion.

The lovely old church stands between two busy highways that take tourists from the North to the South. Travelers who stop to admire it and to inquire about its history are inspired, not only by its architecture, but by the story of the slave whose unselfishness and loyalty to a bargain was responsible for its building.

—HARRIET HENTZ HOUSER

Historic Churches of the South

ST. JAMES
EPISCOPAL
CHURCH

WILMINGTON,
NORTH CAROLINA

WELL KNOWN for its historical landmarks and stately old homes, Wilmington, North Carolina, is equally proud of its many beautiful churches, the oldest of which is St. James Episcopal.

The earliest information on St. James Parish carries us back to the year 1729, when the parish is thought to have been established. North Carolina was a new province at that time and was not adequately supplied with churches. This situation was brought to the attention of a strong religious group in England which arranged to establish the parish in New Hanover County and provide it with a minister. Since Wilmington was then a village of only a few houses facing on the Cape Fear River, the parish took in the entire county.

The first minister on record was the Reverend Richard Marsden, who came from South Carolina. His service began in 1738, and in 1740 he was replaced by the Reverend Mr. Moir. The fortunes of the parish continued to rise and fall with events in the province and across the sea. Several ministers followed Mr. Moir, and the congregation continued to hold its services in the county courthouse. Plans for building a church were discussed through the years, but no action was taken.

In 1749, the people of Wilmington and nearby Brunswick were faced with an unexpected danger when a band of pirates sailed up the river bent on plundering the towns. The entire countryside rose to the challenge, and during the battle which followed, the pirates were beaten off and one of their ships blown up. Large

An unusual art treasure, a painting of the Savior in His passion taken from a pirate ship, hangs in St. James Episcopal Church in Wilmington.

amounts of spoils were taken by the victors, and some of these riches were added to the church building fund. Among the treasures was a painting of the Savior in one of the scenes of His passion. A strange thing to be found on a pirate vessel, this "Ecce Homo"—believed to be by Pacheco—now hangs in the vestry room of the church.

About 1751, actual plans were drawn up for the first church building, with a townsman donating land on the corner of Fourth and Market Streets for a burying ground, and the province authorizing the use of adjoining property on Market Street for the building site. This was then at the edge of town, but is now near the heart of the business district. An architect from a northern province was engaged and the building was begun—Wilmington's first church. However, construction was slow and difficult, for money and supplies were far from plentiful and transportation was extremely poor.

In 1755, the parish received a large donation of Bibles, prayer books, and other religious books from England. A few of these old volumes, bearing the royal coat of arms and the words, "the gift of His Royal Highness, George, Prince of Wales," are still in the church library.

Almost nineteen years elapsed before St. James was completed. A large, square brick building, it had neither steeple nor belfry; at this time, and for some years afterward, the town bell was used to call people to worship. The aisles of the church were paved with square brick and the high reading desk and higher pulpit looked down on huge English-style pews.

These years were troubled ones for the colonies, and it was soon evident that a war with England was inevitable. The last minister to serve the parish before the war resigned about 1775 and was not replaced for nearly 20 years. Five years later, in 1780, Wilmington was taken for British headquarters and the newly built church was almost destroyed. The enclosure around the graveyard was burned and the church was stripped of all furnishings and turned into a hospital—a fate which it was to suffer again during the War Between the States. General Cornwallis himself took over the large, colonial home across from the church —known for many years thereafter as the Cornwallis Mansion.

Some 20 years later, a Dr. Halling came to Wilmington and reorganized the parish. As best they could, the parishioners refurnished the church, and they continued to hold services there until 1839. At that time, the old building was torn down and the present church was erected on the corner of Third and Market facing the river. The whole city is justly proud of this beautiful building. Repaired and partially refurnished several times, St. James contains some unique features, as well as an overall aura of beauty, solemnity and warmth. The huge marble font is covered by a solid oak top, elaborately carved and suspended from the ceiling. The gray walls catch the reflections of the delicate hues of the stained glass windows. A slave gallery, backing the balcony, is a silent reminder of days past. Perhaps the most unusual feature of the church, and certainly the most impressively lovely, is the reredos which backs the altar. It was handcarved by Silas McBee, of Lincolnton, and his two daughters.

In spite of numerous hardships, St. James was established, maintained and stands today, a tribute to the faith and courage which held the parish together and made possible this great church—"the Church of the living God, the pillar and ground of the truth."

—BARBARA SELLERS PATTERSON

Historic Churches of the South

OLD ROCK BAPTIST CHURCH

INDEPENDENCE, TEXAS

IN THE CENTER of the quiet little Texas town of Independence stands Old Rock Church, the oldest Baptist church building still in use in Texas and one of the state's historic shrines. It is a low, unpretentious structure made of native stone with two simple entrances opening into a large, single-room interior.

Old Rock Church dates from the early days of the Texas Republic and many of the great and near-great men of Texas history attended its services. On Sunday, November 19, 1854, General Sam Houston, the father of Texas independence, joined the church and was baptized in Rocky Creek just south of town. His wife and his mother-in-law, Mrs. Nancy Lea, along with several family servants, are buried in the Houston family cemetery across the road from the church.

Sam Houston spent many of his Texas years in and near Washington and Independence, and he had many personal friends in the region. As President of the Republic, he lived in the White House near Washington-on-the-Brazos. He spent a great deal of time visiting on the Lea plantation with his wife's family. Mrs. Nancy Lea, a venerable matriarch, gave the family silver to Old Rock Church to be cast into a bell which was hung in a tower in the churchyard. Through the years she remained a staunch supporter of the causes the old church championed.

Independence was founded in 1836 and its name commemorates the signing of the Texas Declaration of Independence in nearby Washington, capital city of Texas at the time. During its first 50 23 ...

Old Rock Baptist Church is associated with noted names and events in Texas history. Sam Houston, father of Texas independence, was baptized here; it was here that plans were made for building Baylor University.

years, the little town prospered. Frame and stone buildings went up along the business streets, and in the center of town the Masonic Lodge erected a large hall. Up and down the residential streets handsome, dignified homes showed the influence of the Old South. Large plantations surrounded the town.

The church was completed in 1839. In another area it might not be considered an "old" church, since American churches built two centuries earlier are still in use. But during the colonization era, the Mexican government had barred Protestantism in Texas. The Imperial Colonization Law of 1823 was explicit in stating that the Mexican government would "protect the liberty, property, and civil rights of all foreigners who profess the Catholic religion, the established religion of the empire." This law accounts, to a great extent, for the fact that even the oldest of Protestant churches in Texas are young in comparison with the Catholic missions and with the Protestant churches east of the Mississippi River.

During these years the Protestant ministers who came to preach in Texas often carried a rifle under one arm, a Bible under the other. They traveled on horseback through the piney woods, the sagebrush and the cacti, stopping to give spiritual aid to the friendly families along the way. Illness, fatigue and physical danger took their toll. Some of them landed in jail for their activities.

In the Austin colony, during the 1820's, eleven Baptist families met secretly with the Reverend Daniel Parker. On several occasions the officials of the Mexican government closed their eyes to his activities, but after he organized a Sunday school he was finally arrested. He was forced to leave the colony and went to Illinois where, in 1833, he organized a church which he promptly set about transferring to Texas. His trip back to Austin's Colony is a famous chapter in the history of the Baptist Church in Texas. The congregation had no regular meeting place until 1839, when Parker built a log house which was known as the Pilgrim Church of Pedestinarian Regular Baptists. The original building is no longer in existence.

In a special way, Old Rock Church is a memorial to this eventful era in the history of the Baptist Church.

It was in this church that plans were made for building Baylor University, and members of the first Baylor faculty worshipped here. In the early 1840's Baptist dignitaries met in the church to consider plans to build the school on a site just south of town. Money was raised, small buildings erected, and in 1845 Baylor University accepted its first student registrations under a charter issued by the Republic of Texas.

The school remained in Independence until 1886 when Dr. Rufus C. Burleson, president, combined it with the Baptist school in Waco and moved the institution to that city. Crumbling brick walls are all that remain today of Baylor's proud beginning in Independence, but the school has fulfilled the hopes of its founders and is one of the largest denominational institutions in the South.

Today Independence is a quiet place with recollections of an exciting past. Some of the sons and daughters of the pioneers who founded the town still live in this section, and many pioneer family names appear on the church rolls. Old Rock Church is proud of its place in local history, but its first concern is, as it has always been, to render service in the present.

Historic Churches of the South

THE CHURCH
OF THE
POINTING FINGER

THE GENERAL drew his horse to a stop on a knoll overlooking the sleepy, peaceful village and sat gazing thoughtfully at the many church spires which rose above the tops of giant trees. Turning to an aide after a moment, he declared, "This town is too beautiful to destroy!"

Historic Churches of the South

So it happened that Port Gibson, Mississippi, was spared the torch when, in a skirmish preliminary to the siege of Vicksburg, General Ulysses S. Grant and his troops occupied the town.

Members of the First Presbyterian Church felt that the unique steeple which graced their building had done much to influence the general's decision. That steeple did undoubtedly catch his eye, as it has caught the eyes of thousands of travelers from all over the nation for nearly a hundred years.

The First Presbyterian Church is one of the most unusual houses of worship in the entire South, and its most striking physical feature is the steeple tipped by a clenched fist with the forefinger pointing heavenward. In southwest Mississippi "the church with the steeple-finger" is a landmark as well known as the Vicksburg National Park, which lies a few miles to the north.

Inside the building hang chandeliers which once lighted the proud old Mississippi River steamer, the "Robert E. Lee." The "Lee's" owners, who were members of the church, donated the chandeliers when the river craft was electrified in the early 1880's. These lighting fixtures, which have themselves since been wired for electricity, are decorated with tiny wood carvings of General Lee astride his warhorse, Traveler.

27 . . .

The unique steeple of the First Presbyterian Church of Port Gibson, better known as "the Church of the Pointing Finger," is a famous landmark.

The church was established in 1807 by three missionaries from South Carolina who came to the Mississippi frontier down the Natchez Trace. It was first known as the Bayou Pierre Presbyterian Church. In 1828, it was moved to its present site, bringing it nearer to the center of population, and the less picturesque name was adopted. At the same time, the church acquired its first regular pastor, the Reverend Dr. Zebulon Butler. Before this, the church evidently had been served by lay members, a practice common in pioneer days.

Dr. Butler was a redoubtable figure of a man, and his favorite pulpit gesture was the finger pointing sternly to Heaven. Church members perpetuated the gesture in the finial of their steeple as a tribute to this man who devoted his entire ministry—32 years—to their church.

The original hand was carved of wood by Daniel Foley, who went on to achieve fame in Italy as a painter, and it was embellished with a layer of gold leaf. Eventually this glittering symbol was damaged by weather, bees and woodpeckers, and around 1900 a new hand was cast in metal. From its pedestal, it measures fourteen feet, and a man can stand in its six-foot index finger.

The record of long service set by the church's first pastor has continued, generally. Since 1828, the church has had only nine ministers; however, only one of these men—the Reverend H. D. Brownlee, who was pastor of First Presbyterian for 36 years—served the church longer than did Dr. Butler. This record of long tenure in the pulpit suggests that the congregation has perhaps been inspired, or at least uncommonly fortunate, in selecting its pastors—and also that the congregation itself has shown an exemplary spirit of cooperation.

The hand on the steeple has attracted many visitors, including the late Robert L. Ripley, who featured the church in his popular "Believe It or Not" cartoon. Tourists from all over the United States have left their impressions in the church's guest register, but perhaps the most representative comment is the one contained in a letter from a Methodist minister from Connecticut. He wrote:

"The people of Port Gibson identify this church as Presbyterian, but to travelers like myself, it can be nothing but 'the church with the finger of God.'"

—ROGER THAMES

CANE RIDGE
MEETING HOUSE

OLD CANE RIDGE Meeting House, located near Paris, Kentucky, was built in 1791, when Kentucky was frontier country and settlements were small and isolated.

Daniel Boone, First Citizen of Kentucky, called this section around Paris his favorite hunting ground. After one of his famous trips he went back to his Pennsylvania home and urged some of his friends to accompany him on his next journey south.

One of his neighbors, Robert W. Finley, was so impressed by Boone's tales that in 1784 he organized a hunting party and explored the region under Boone's guidance. He came home full of plans to move to the territory and establish a frontier settlement.

In 1789, Finley left Pennsylvania accompanied by a group of pioneers bound for Kentucky. They settled at Cane Ridge, built homes, and began to cultivate the land. They were soon joined by a large group of North Carolina settlers who had heard of Robert Finley and his activities as a preacher and a schoolmaster.

Late in that first year the people decided to build a church. They selected a site and marked the finest trees on the ridge for building material. During the building period parties of men went into the woods to fell the trees, notching them on the spot. Sometimes it was necessary for them to climb the tallest trees to locate the church site and find their way back, as canebrakes in Kentucky in that era often grew to a height of ten feet.

Finley thought that the church should have a gallery similar to the ones back home. And so Cane Ridge Meeting House had a 31 ...

Cane Ridge Meeting House is the "birthplace of the Christian Church."

gallery, a most unusual one. It was entered from the outside by a ladder. The log structure was about fifty feet long and thirty feet wide, with a rude pulpit and log benches set on smooth tree trunks.

From the very beginning it was an active church with a large membership for that day and time. Soon after the meeting house was finished, Robert Finley built a seminary which he called the Cane Ridge Log Cabin Seminary. It was located about a quarter of a mile from the church near a fine spring that is known today, fittingly enough, as Finley's Spring. The seminary was in session for five terms and the student body grew so rapidly that there was talk of adding another building. During the fifth year, however, a bolt of lightning struck the building and the ensuing fire burned it to the ground. The seminary was never reopened, but the fragments of the old foundation can still be seen.

During Finley's ministry the meeting house was Presbyterian. In 1796, depressed by the loss of the school and eager to pioneer another frontier, Finley left Cane Ridge for Ohio, and the Reverend Barton W. Stone came from Virginia to take his place.

Stone was a reformer and was one of the originators of the movement which led to the founding of the Disciples of Christ. In 1804, he and five fellow ministers of the Presbyterian Church dissolved the Springfield Presbytery, and Stone first proclaimed publicly the principles that gave birth to the Christian Church, as the Disciples' church is generally known.

Stone served Cane Ridge Meeting House until 1811. He was followed in about five years by Thomas Campbell, also a reformer, and then by Alexander Campbell, Thomas Campbell's son. Gradually these men realized how much their movements had in common, and the unification of the two factions began in Lexington, Kentucky, on January 1, 1832. Stone is given much of the credit for this unification, and Cane Ridge Meeting House is known as the birthplace of the Christian Church.

Throughout these turbulent years, however, the meeting house was used by all of the people of the area. A church document dated February 12, 1829, shows that it was used by both Presbyterians and members of the new Christian Church, and "was free for other societies to worship in when not occupied by these churches."

In 1829, the people of Cane Ridge decided that they should repair and remodel the church. The gallery was removed, the walls weather-boarded, the interior plastered, a ceiling added and new benches installed. Again in 1882 repairs were made. The interior was painted and comfortable pews were installed.

Then in 1932, the hundredth anniversary of the union of the Stone and Campbell movements, old Cane Ridge Meeting House was restored to its primitive appearance. The weather-boarding was removed and the old logs again exposed. The interior was also restored to its former state.

To the east of the church is the cemetery in which are buried many of the pioneer citizens of the region, including the Reverend Mr. Stone.

Besides being known as one of the fathers of the Christian Church, Stone is remembered to this day for his part in the organization of the Great Revival. Late in the summer of 1801 between twenty and thirty thousand people, so the records say, came together at Cane Ridge Meeting House to hold a great union revival. Many of them lived near the ridge, but some of them came from Ohio, and a great many families traveled several hundred miles to attend the series of meetings. The roads were packed with carriages and wagons, and campfires lighted the ridge each evening as the folks gathered to worship and to visit. Temporary pulpits were built, and sometimes as many as seven ministers were preaching at the same time. More than three thousand conversions were recorded. It was many years before the attendance record for the Great Revival was surpassed.

Services were recently discontinued in Cane Ridge Meeting House because of the serious deterioration of several parts of the building, but the historic old structure is being preserved as a shrine by the Disciples of Christ. And visitors from all over the United States stop by to see this little log church built 161 years ago by men who were not afraid to cross frontiers.

Historic Churches of the South

ST. LOUIS CATHEDRAL

NEW ORLEANS, LOUISIANA

Historic Churches of the South

EVER SINCE the French set up a provincial government in the crescent-shaped bend of the Mississippi, New Orleans' Jackson Square, then known as the Place d'Armes, has been a center of activity. Here, facing the square and the river, early settlers built their first rude house of worship, which they called St. Louis Church in honor of the patron saint of Bourbon France. Today, St. Louis Cathedral, one of North America's most famous landmarks, still stands facing the square and the industrial area which lines the docks along the river.

That first colonial church was destroyed by hurricane on September 11, 1722, and for several years its parishioners were forced to worship in a rented house while they saved funds for the church they planned to build on the old site. There were no pews or seats in the small house, so on Sundays and feast days the state officials and other well-to-do citizens went to church accompanied by servants carrying chairs.

Work began on the second church in 1724 but was not completed until three years later. The outside walls of the new church were of brick and wood covered with adobe plaster. It was a splendid structure for that day, and its tower and belfry made it a landmark on the Mississippi. It had an organ and choir loft, and there were special seats for the governor, the treasurer, the members of the council, and military officials. Because it was centrally located and frequented by persons from all walks of life, all official governmental announcements were posted on the doorway which faced the Place d'Armes.

One of the most memorable services conducted in St. Louis Cathedral was the thanksgiving service held after the victorious Battle of New Orleans.

...36

After France ceded Louisiana to Spain, Padre Cyrillo de Barcelona, a Spanish friar, was appointed to the position of Auxiliary Bishop of St. Louis. New Orleans was growing rapidly in those days, and the church continued to expand until it was destroyed by the great fire which virtually wiped out the city on Good Friday of 1788.

Rebuilding the church looked like an almost impossible task, for the parishioners also had their homes and business houses to replace. But a wealthy citizen, Don Andres Almonaster y Roxas, came forward and offered to build a new church from his own funds. He had come to New Orleans penniless some twenty years earlier, but in the meanwhile had managed to amass a great fortune. He had already done much for the city that had made him rich. His gifts included the Hospital of San Lazaro for lepers, the Hospital of San Carlos de Caridad, and the Chapel of the Ursuline Convent. He was ambitious for power and demanded certain political privileges in exchange for the gift of the building. His offer was finally accepted, but not before it had given rise to much bickering and dissention.

The building was finished in 1794. Don Andres Almonaster died on April 26, 1798, and was buried in the parish cemetery. A year and a half later his remains were placed under a marble slab in the church in front of the Altar of St. Francis.

St. Louis became a Cathedral in April 1793, but the first bishop of Louisiana, Don Luis de Penalver y Cardenas, did not arrive until 1795.

On December 1, 1803, the old cathedral witnessed the ceremony in the Place d'Armes when the royal red and yellow flag of Spain was replaced by the tricolor of Napoleon's France. Twenty days later that emblem was removed and replaced by the banner of the United States with its fifteen stars and fifteen stripes.

In this same square huge crowds feted General Andrew Jackson after the battle of New Orleans, and surged into the cathedral to attend the memorable thanksgiving service held in his honor.

The old church built by Don Andres has been repaired and enlarged many times, but it has never been wholly rebuilt. In 1814 the facade was changed and the low hexagonal towers were crowned with spires. Some ten years later the central tower was added. In 1850, just before the Place d'Armes became Jackson Square, the central tower fell, smashing part of the roof and the walls. The present facade with its columns and pilasters dates from that year.

In 1881, the church was repaired and enlarged with funds which were subscribed locally and supplemented by a substantial donation from France.

At that time the paintings on the walls and the dome were restored. Erasme Humbrecht, a famous church painter, restored these paintings, replaced some of the faded ones, and added some original murals. These works of religious art are the glory of the present cathedral.

Old St. Louis Cathedral cannot claim the magnificence or architectural beauty of some of our other famous churches, but it has a firm hold on the hearts of the people of New Orleans. No sightseeing tour of the Crescent City is complete without a visit to this historic landmark.

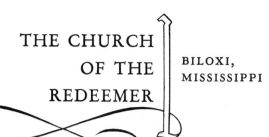

THE CHURCH OF THE REDEEMER

BILOXI, MISSISSIPPI

Historic Churches of the South

SET UNDER great oaks festooned with Spanish moss stands the little red brick Church of the Redeemer, which has a significant place in the history of the South because of its close connection with Jefferson Davis and his family. Its story dates back to the late 1840's. Records of those early days are sketchy, but it is known that services were held in Biloxi by visiting clergymen of the Episcopal Church, and apparently there was a local organization of sorts.

From 1849 to 1854, the Reverend Thomas S. Savage regularly held services in Biloxi and other towns along the Gulf Coast. Then, in 1854, the state legislature chartered and organized the parish, and the church acquired a resident rector. (The parish celebrated its hundredth anniversary in 1949, however, as it is considered to have started as an organized mission with the advent of the Reverend Mr. Savage.) One of the vestrymen of the church was the future president of the Confederacy.

The original church building was a frame structure on the corner of Howard Avenue and Nixon Street. It was used until 1892, when Harry T. Howard, a prominent Biloxi businessman, donated a tract of land at East Beach and Bellman Streets and built the present church as a memorial to the Reverend R. G. Hinsdale, who served the parish from 1883 to 1889. The old frame building was deconsecrated and moved to the rear of the new brick one. It was subsequently enlarged and remodeled for use as a parish house, and today is the hub of many religious and community activities. In its tower hangs a bell which tradition says came from a small chapel 39...

The Church of the Redeemer in Biloxi is closely associated with the names of Jefferson Davis and three distinguished Confederate generals.

... 40

on an ante-bellum plantation; it is used to announce the opening of Sunday school.

The present church building is filled with mementos of Jefferson Davis and his family. Just inside the doorway, to the left, hangs a framed letter dated June 3, 1888, from Mr. Davis to the Reverend Mr. Hinsdale. It reads:

"Enclosed I send a contribution, a small sum which you must regard not as the measure of my will, but of my ability.

"To you is made the confession that circumstances have made me poorer than an average fisherman, but other demands are here subordinate to the cause of Him who died for the redemption of fallen man."

To the right of the doorway is the pew which Mr. Davis and his family occupied during the time they lived at Beauvoir. It is draped with a silk Confederate flag and is marked with a silver nameplate.

The six beautiful stained glass windows in the nave were made in Munich over fifty years ago by a celebrated artist. Three of these windows are memorials to Jefferson Davis, his wife, and his younger daughter, Winnie, and were donated by the Daughters of the Confederacy. The altar, also given by the Daughters of the Confederacy, is a memorial to the Davises' older daughter, Mrs. Margaret Howell Davis Hays. Mrs. Hays herself contributed a window as a memorial to her four brothers.

When Varina Davis was at the point of death, she asked her daughter Margaret to send her diamond ring as a last gift to the Church of the Redeemer. After her mother died, Mrs. Hays wrote to the rector to tell him of the bequest. She explained, however, that she wished to keep the ring because Mrs. Davis had worn it for many years, and she asked if, in its place, she might give the church a silver Communion service.

Church officials agreed to Mrs. Hays' request, and she sent a five-piece sterling silver service. On the chalice is engraved, "I will receive the cup of salvation, and call upon the name of the Lord. Varina Howell Davis, May 7, 1826—October 16, 1906." The large flagon bears the inscription, "My soul is athirst for God, yea even for the living God. Jefferson Davis, June 3, 1808—December 16, 1889." The paten is inscribed in memory of the sons of Jefferson and Varina Davis.

Silver plates mark the pews of three distinguished Confederate generals who regularly attended services at the Church of the Redeemer. They were Lieutenant General Alexander P. Stewart, who after the war served as chancellor for the University of Mississippi before coming to Biloxi to live; Brigadier General Joseph Davis, nephew of Jefferson Davis and postmaster of Biloxi for many years; and Brigadier General Samuel W. Ferguson, who received the keys at the surrender of Fort Sumter.

Just inside the entrance to the church, the Episcopal flag and the United Nations flag are on display, along with seven flags which have flown over Biloxi—the flags of France, England, Spain, the United States, the Confederacy, the Magnolia flag (which was the official flag of the State of Mississippi before the War Between the States), and the present official state flag (which is an adaptation of the Confederate flag). All are authentic flags of their period and were dedicated at a special service.

At the front of the church—and matching the Munich windows in the nave—is a three-panel stained glass memorial window which was dedicated on Easter Sunday, 1946. The inscription on this window reads: "The Confederacy, 1861-1865. And a tribute to the spirit of the South, which has contributed high devotion to an ideal, courageous valour and gentleness of living to our American Way of Life." Money for the window was donated by church members and other citizens of Biloxi.

On the church grounds stands a massive live oak with widespread branches, one of which is twisted into the shape of a ring.

Legend has it that the daughter of a Biloxi chief loved the chief of an enemy tribe. Her father, greatly displeased at this turn of events, vowed, "My daughter shall never wed a brave from a hostile tribe until a ring grows in yonder oak." During the night there was a violent storm, and the next morning the father saw that the winds had twisted a branch of the young tree into a perfect ring. Feeling that nature had conspired to help the young lovers, he gave his blessing to their marriage.

Every day the Church of the Redeemer opens its doors to all who would come in. The present rector, the Reverend Edward A. DeMiller, who has served the church for thirty years, says, "We invite the wayfarer to come in and find peace within the hallowed walls of the Church of the Redeemer."

—ANN MORETON

Historic Churches of the South

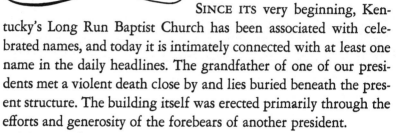

LONG RUN
BAPTIST
CHURCH

JEFFERSON COUNTY,
KENTUCKY

Historic
Churches
of the
South

SINCE ITS very beginning, Kentucky's Long Run Baptist Church has been associated with celebrated names, and today it is intimately connected with at least one name in the daily headlines. The grandfather of one of our presidents met a violent death close by and lies buried beneath the present structure. The building itself was erected primarily through the efforts and generosity of the forebears of another president.

The story begins in 1780, when Morgan Hughes, with a party predominately Quaker and Baptist, came into central Kentucky and settled near a pleasant little stream at the east end of Jefferson County. The original survey for his station, or fort, was made by Squire Boone, Daniel's brother. When one of the surveying party was interrupted at his work and pursued for a great distance by Indians, the little creek gained its name, Long Run.

Hughes' Station was a weak fort, according to contemporary historians, affording little protection against the hostile neighboring redskins. However, poorly built as they were, its cabins and blockhouses were enough to induce Captain Abraham Linkhorn to bring his wife and family there to settle a 400-acre grant of land adjoining the little settlement. With the help of his three boys, he built a small cabin on his land—though the family continued to live at the fort—and "put in" a crop. He never lived to harvest the crop, however, for one day as he worked with his sons in the field, he was felled by a shot from the nearby woods.

Fourteen-year-old Mordecai, the eldest boy, quickly sent Josiah, twelve, to the fort for help and then retreated to the cabin. Eight-

Grandparents of Abraham Lincoln and Harry S. Truman played important roles in the colorful history of Kentucky's Long Run Baptist Church.

year-old Thomas remained crouching by his father's body. Mordecai, in the cabin, was able to avenge his father's death and save his small brother's life, for his first rifle shot killed the Indian who came stealing up to his victim's side. Josiah returned with men from the fort and, after a short skirmish, the Indian party was routed.

The "Widow Linkhorn" buried her husband in the dooryard of the little cabin and stayed on at the fort with her children until they could harvest the crop. They then moved to Washington County, where the boys grew to manhood. Thomas Lincoln, as the name was now recorded, married Nancy Hanks and moved again, this time to Hardin County. When, three years later, their baby boy was born, he was named Abraham for his grandfather.

The Linkhorn cabin apparently never was occupied as a home,

and the settlers of Hughes' Station soon began using it as a meeting house and schoolhouse. As early as 1780, community meetings were held there, probably before the Linkhorns left the fort. By 1797 the Baptists outnumbered the Quakers, and the cabin housed a constituted Baptist church, which took its name from nearby Long Run Creek.

By 1803, a stone building had replaced the cabin, and the church had 57 members. John Penny was probably its first regular pastor, though records are not definite on this point. Kentucky's first Baptist Association was formed here in 1804, taking in 24 churches and 1,619 members. It, too, was called by the name of the little creek. When the building was enlarged, Linkhorn's grave was covered over.

The following year, the little church which had weathered the perils of the wilderness was almost wrecked on the dangers of dogma. At a log-rolling in the neighborhood, a debate arose over the old question, Is an untruth ever justified? There was propounded what at that time must have been a most realistic example: Suppose a man had five children. Four of them are killed by the Indians, but he succeeds in hiding the fifth in the woods nearby. The Indians ask him if he has any other children. Is he justified in telling them he has not?

The dispute grew so warm that eventually the whole congregation became engaged in it. The "Lying Party" left the church, moved three or four miles west and, with seven members, founded the Flat Rock Baptist Church in March 1805.

In the years to follow, the membership of the Long Run Church fluctuated, increased by revivals, decreased by the sending out of members to form new churches. It was thus "mother church" to several new churches: in 1812, Dover Church; in 1827, Floyd's Fork Church, later known as the Fisherville Baptist Church; and in 1872, Pewee Valley Church.

Though one historian notes that during the period between 1842 and 1861 the church "did not prosper," and—whether as cause or effect—pastors were changed seven times, something was accomplished which is a milestone in the history of any church, large or small: a new building was erected.

During the month of October 1844, the old stone meeting house was razed; the following year a new brick church was built, using the historic old stones as its foundation. The building today stands virtually unchanged.

The family whose name was most outstanding in the church records in 1844 were the Greggs. William Gregg served on the building committee, while John Gregg, his brother, was treasurer of the project. They contributed more than their leadership. The bricks were fired on the old Gregg place and donated, along with much of the labor, by the Gregg family. When the church's title to its land proved uncertain, it was a Gregg who gave the land to the church.

One-hundred-and-fiftieth on the church roll of that year was the name of Harriet Louisa Gregg, sister of William and John. Harriet Gregg married Solomon Young, a fellow church member, and with him later moved to Jackson County, Missouri, where in 1852 their daughter Martha Ellen was born. Martha Ellen married John Anderson Truman, and, in 1884, her baby boy was born. He was named Harry, presumably for his grandmother.

The church which owed so much to the Greggs was built with four entrances, two in front and two at the rear. Inside, the hand-made pews, still in use today, were partitioned into four groups, separating male and female, white and black. Separate entrances and seating arrangements for men and women were evidence of Quaker influence, but discrimination between races was not. However, once in the church, Negro slaves had identical rights with their masters, being allowed an equal voice in all church matters. This was Quakerism at its best.

After the slaves were freed, by the grandson of the man whose cabin formed the church's first meeting place, no more Negro members were admitted. Those already in the congregation were retained. The last colored member to die was Edmund Gregg, possibly a descendant of one of the Gregg slaves. He was buried, in 1922, by his fellow members among the Revolutionary War heroes in the little churchyard.

It is interesting to note that Harry S. Truman and Abraham Lincoln, two of our presidents who have been outstanding for their championship of human liberties, should have their roots, ancestrally speaking, in this little church which judged all men equal, "regardless of race, color, or previous condition of servitude," long before the law so judged them.

Today the Long Run Baptist Association, first formed here, has more than tripled its membership. The Long Run Baptist Church is still active, doing its full share of the praiseworthy work carried on by the rural churches of America.

Who can say—some day another president may trace his ancestry to its membership.

—SUE McCLELLAND THIERMAN

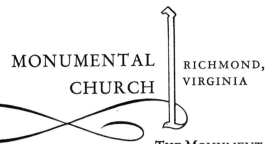

MONUMENTAL CHURCH

RICHMOND, VIRGINIA

THE MONUMENTAL CHURCH in Richmond, as its name implies, was built as a memorial. On the evening of December 26, 1811, in the theater which then stood on the church site, a large and distinguished audience gathered to witness the Placide Stock Company's performance of two plays— "The Father, or Family Feuds," and "Raymond and Agnes, or The Bleeding Nun."

During the second act, fire broke out behind the scenes and spread rapidly, blocking all the exits. Among the 72 who died in the holocaust were George William Smith, governor of the state, and A. B. Venable, president of the Bank of Virginia. The tragedy affected almost every home in the city. Condolences poured in from all parts of the United States and Europe, and members of the U. S. Senate wore mourning bands for thirty days.

On the day following the calamity, Richmond citizens held a mass meeting and appointed Chief Justice John Marshall chairman of a committee to collect funds to build a memorial to those who perished in the fire. By order of the Common Hall, known today as the City Council, the city purchased the site of the theater "to be consecrated as the sacred deposit of the ashes of the victims and enclose it within suitable walls of brick."

After much deliberation, it was decided that the memorial should take the form of a church. The city gave the site and $5,000 to the building fund; citizens of Richmond, poor and rich alike, subscribed generously to the cause.

Robert Mills, an eminent architect of the day, was commissioned 49 . . .

Monumental Church in Richmond was built on the site of a tragic fire.

to draw the plans. An original thinker, he designed a building which resembles a museum or library far more than it does the conventional church architecture of its day.

"Old Monumental," as it is now known, set a standard in design that was followed in Richmond for many years. Today, this church and Valentine Museum, formerly the Wickham home, are the only remaining examples of architect Mills' creative genius.

Before the church was built, the construction committee had engravings made from the architect's drawings, and these aquatints have been found hanging in homes in France and in many parts of the East as well as in the States. These pictures show the church with the tower and steeple which were in the original plans but were never built.

The cornerstone of the church was laid on August 1, 1812, and ...50 the first service was held on May 4, 1814. Within the porch is a marble shaft surmounted by an urn on which are inscribed the names of those whose ashes lie in the brick vault beneath the floor.

The Monumental Church became an Episcopal church because the majority of the building fund subscribers and purchasers of pews were Episcopalians, but it is cherished by the whole city.

Many prominent men of Virginia have contributed to the growth of Old Monumental. Bishop Channing Moore was the first rector; Chief Justice Marshall was a regular communicant. Edgar Allan Poe attended services here when he was a boy. George D. Fisher, long-time vestryman, recorded the annals of the church in a volume, *History and Reminiscences of the Monumental Church, 1814-1878,* which contains much material of value to present day historians.

In 1920, the Association for the Preservation of Virginia Antiquities placed a tablet on the outside wall of the church. It relates the fact that in a building not far from this site on Academy Square, the Virginia Convention of 1788 met and ratified the Constitution of the United States.

Services have been held regularly in Monumental Church since its opening in 1814. There have been several long rectorships in these 138 years; the twelfth and present rector, the Reverend George Ossman, has served the church for twenty-one years.

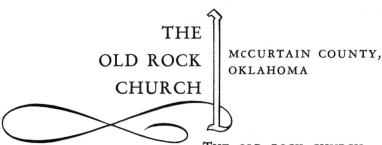

THE OLD ROCK CHURCH

MCCURTAIN COUNTY, OKLAHOMA

THE OLD ROCK CHURCH near Millerton, the oldest church building in Oklahoma and one of the state's most famous landmarks, stands as a monument to the Reverend Alfred Wright, a pioneer missionary to the Indians, who organized the church nearly 120 years ago.

The Reverend Mr. Wright, ordained as a Presbyterian minister at Charleston, South Carolina, in 1819, was first sent to Mississippi as a missionary to the Choctaw Indians. He made his headquarters at Goshen station among the Six Town Clan—a subdivision of the Choctaw tribe—and soon he had an outpost among this same clan near the Alabama border. By 1828 there were 40 missionaries working among the Choctaws in Mississippi, but with negligible results. Then a wave of spiritual enthusiasm swept the tribe, and the task of Christianizing the Indians in that area would have been accomplished in short order but for the tragedy of the Great Removal to what is now the state of Oklahoma.

By the Treaty of Dancing Rabbit Creek, signed in 1830, the Choctaws ceded to the United States nearly 19 million acres in Mississippi and Alabama in return for 20 million acres in the Indian Territory and $2,225,000 in money and goods. The Choctaws began their great migration in 1831, moving by ox teams and flatboats. The trip was extremely difficult, and so many of the Indians died on the way that the road came to be known as the Trail of Tears.

Before they moved, the Six Town Clan had an understanding with their missionary that he was to join them in their new home.

The Old Rock Church, the oldest church building in Oklahoma, was constructed nearly 110 years ago by a pioneer missionary to the Indians.

Wright went East to get religious literature printed, and after that was ill for some time, so it was not until late in 1832 that he rejoined his scattered flock and selected a mission site, which he named Wheelock in memory of his friend, Eleazer Wheelock, the founder of Dartmouth College.

Dr. W. B. Morrison, in his book *The Red Man's Trail,* gives this vivid picture of the reorganization of the Indian church:

" . . . on Sunday, December 9, 1832, under a large tree . . . the first service was held. . . . The underbrush had been cleared away and a few split-log benches prepared. Dr. Wright used a common wooden box for a pulpit. It was a novel sight to see the Indians coming out of the overgrown wilderness to attend the service, the men with their long black hair and colored blankets and the women wearing dresses of tanned deer hide and moccasins. . . . The 53 . . .

service opened with the singing of the Choctaw hymns learned in the old home in Mississippi. They were sung now with an unusual tinge of sadness. . . . Wright's sermon was heard with much attention, and . . . at the conclusion . . . thirty of the old members and seven new ones were received into the new Wheelock church."

In 1843, Wright established a boarding school at Wheelock, but it was not until 1846 that the pastor and his flock were able to erect a church building. Stone was used because "the people wanted a lasting monument to the planting of religion and civilization in the West."

Wright died in 1853 and is buried near his church.

The American Board of Commissioners for Foreign Missions withdrew its support of Wheelock in 1859 because of the slavery controversy; the missionaries had generally adopted a neutral policy that was not easily understood by the home offices in the North. With the outbreak of the War Between the States in 1861, Wheelock mission and the boarding school were suspended altogether because of the charge that the minister, the Reverend John Edwards, was an abolition agent.

During the war, the church building was used by soldiers; then in 1869 it burned, leaving only the stone walls standing. For fifteen years, the mission site was a desolate place, unfrequented except for an occasional religious service in the old log school house, and trees grew within the thick stone walls. Then in 1884 John Edwards returned to Wheelock and repaired and reopened the school. In 1887 the church building was restored, and it was used regularly for a number of years.

Around the turn of the century, the church building once more fell into disuse except for an occasional service. But in 1942 the First Presbyterian Church of nearby Idabel opened a Sunday school in Wheelock mission and, as the Sunday school grew, the community again became interested in the church. On December 14, 1946, a new Wheelock Presbyterian Church was organized, largely through the efforts of the Reverend R. R. Craig, pastor of the First Presbyterian Church of Idabel. The church is now serving the spiritual interests of a good farm community and the students of Wheelock Academy, a school for Indian girls.

—Mary Lorraine Smith

Historic Churches of the South

ST. MICHAEL'S | CHARLESTON, SOUTH CAROLINA

ASK ANY CHARLESTONIAN what he considers the most familiar sound in his native city and more than likely his answer will be "the bells of St. Michael's." Few sets of bells can claim so eventful a past or so firm a hold on the heart of a city.

Their story begins in 1764, when they were imported from England along with a clock. The eight bells made a second journey across the Atlantic when the British, after the surrender of Charleston during the Revolution, took them to London as spoils of war. A former Charleston merchant learned of their fate, searched them out, bought them and shipped them back. When the ship arrived at the dock, the townspeople, overjoyed to have the bells back again, clambered aboard and dragged them away. They carried the bells to the steeple and rehung them immediately. Grateful Charlestonians reimbursed the merchant from funds raised through popular subscription.

During the early days of the War Between the States the bells again left St. Michael's. This time they were sent by the parish to Columbia to be melted and made into ammunition. They were not used, but Sherman's men found them on their march through South Carolina and smashed them. The fragments were collected, however, and finally returned to the church.

These fragments were sent to the firm of London bellmakers who had made the bells. They were melted and recast with new metal, in the original molds. Their fifth voyage across the Atlantic brought them back to St. Michael's. From that day until this they

St. Michael's Church is one of Charleston's most impressive landmarks.

have chimed the hours and called people to worship without interruption.

The cornerstone of St. Michael's was laid in 1752, but the church was not opened for services until 1761. The name of the architect is not known, although the church is built in the tradition of Sir Christopher Wren. Except for the addition of the sacristy in 1883, the structure of the building has not been changed. The interior was designed to carry out worship according to the Book of Common Prayer, and St. Michael's is one of the few city churches in the United States to retain this original design.

The stucco-covered brick structure, 130 feet in length and 60 feet wide, has a slate roof and a 168-foot wooden belfry. On the top of the steeple is a large ball, made of cypress and covered with copper.

In 1865, the church was hit and seriously damaged by a shell from the Federal batteries on Morris Island. The walls were partially destroyed, leaving the church open to the pillagers who ransacked it during Federal occupation of the city. Many of the ornaments were removed.

Visitors are always interested in the beautiful churchyard gates. Set in the handsome brick wall which surrounds the cemetery, these intricate hand-wrought iron gates are a favorite subject for artists and photographers, and are renowned for their design and structural excellence. In the churchyard are graves dating back to 1680. (St. Michael's stands on the site of the first Anglican church built south of Virginia, somewhere around 1680.) An oddity among the monuments is the head of the wooden bedstead in which Mary Ann Luyton died in 1770.

ARKANSAS' OLDEST CHURCH ST. MARY'S

PINE BLUFF, ARKANSAS

THE TIDY LITTLE brick church on Plum Bayou ten miles northeast of Pine Bluff gives little indication to the casual passerby that it is Arkansas' oldest house of worship, built about 1833 to give spiritual nurture to some 50 French Catholic families who had settled along the Arkansas River. Only on the tombstones behind the 25-by-40-foot structure—some of them very old, some quite new—can be read the succeeding chapters in a devotion that has been handed down from the days when Arkansas was not yet a state.

Historic Churches of the South

Before this account turns back to 1833 and one Francis Newismond Vaugine, let us explain how it happens that a church more than a hundred years old has walls of symmetrical white brick and, inside, butane gas heaters and fluorescent lighting. That story is told by the single marker for the graves of Allen White (1888-1927) and his mother, Emma Frances White (1865-1935). Beneath the latter's chiseled name are the words "Patroness and Benefactress of St. Mary's."

As a memorial to her son, Emma Frances Vaugine White secured permission to preserve the church his great-grandfather, the aforementioned Francis Newismond Vaugine, helped to found by a gift of land. Nothing of the original building was removed, but the old walls, said to bear the scars of a skirmish which took place during the War Between the States, were encased in brick. On the inside, the church was plastered and trimmed with woodwork of polished walnut and cedar from trees growing on the church plot.

Mrs. White made St. Mary's the sole beneficiary in her will, and

Despite its modern exterior, little St. Mary's Church near Pine Bluff dates back over 120 years and is the oldest house of worship in Arkansas.

the income from her estate assures lasting care for a shrine that is both personal and historic.

Many names figure in St. Mary's early history. There was Colonel Creed Taylor, husband of Eulalia Vaugine, who gave lumber from his sawmill for construction of the church. There was a Derreseaux family, and another with the name Valliere, and there were Brookses and Burtons and Mitchells. Fathers Duprey, Bole, Paris, Donnelley and Mattingly are among the priests who served at St. Mary's in the early years. But no name appears more often than Vaugine.

One heroic chapter in St. Mary's history is witnessed to by the monument erected in memory of Mother Agnes Hart, member of the Order of the Sisters of Loretto and Superioress of St. Mary's Academy from October 1838 until her death in August 1839 from malnutrition and malaria. One face of the marker tells this concise story: "Buried at St. Mary's on the River August 22, 1839. Remains interred at St. Mary's Church Plum Bayou, May 1869."

Those who have heard the story from their grandparents give a fuller account: The church and an academy operated in connection with it (1838 to 1842) once stood several miles closer to the river—the ever-shifting, sometimes rampaging Arkansas River. When in 1869, caving banks endangered both the church and burial ground, the building was moved some five miles inland to its present site. Graves, including that of Mother Agnes Hart, were opened and their contents carefully transported to the new cemetery. At the time of Mother Hart's death, the rules of her order required that her body be buried without benefit of coffin. But by the time the removal occurred, that rule had been expunged and her remains were carefully placed in a neat coffin for reinterment.

One story goes that the building now standing inside its brick protection at Plum Bayou was built, as early as 1782, at Arkansas Post downstream from St. Mary's Landing, and was later moved by flatboat to the Vaugine land. But neither the church records available to the present rector, the Reverend Thomas F. Walshe, nor the recollections of Mrs. Mary Vaugine Barron, one of the two surviving granddaughters of Francis Vaugine, confirm the legend.

St. Mary's stands today as a mission church with services held on alternate Sundays for across-the-river parishioners of St. Joseph's in Pine Bluff. During the years since it first opened its doors to the people of the countryside, St. Mary's Landing has been dwarfed by nearby Pine Bluff, now a city of many homes and schools and churches and of a bustling commerce streaming along radiating highways.

Meanwhile, little old St. Mary's, in spite of its brave new walls and efficient lighting, has changed but little. With two old cedars guarding its entrance and jays in the honeysuckle along the bayou scolding at mid-week intruders, it seems simply to have remained steadfast—a small outpost of the Mother Church. The visitor has only to turn his back on the traffic whipping along the nearby highway to believe that the bluets and anemones blooming in the churchyard today are the same ones that delighted Celestine Vaugine and Therese Derreseaux and Hiacinthe Tenas a hundred springs ago.

Even to one of another faith, the little white cross old St. Mary's lifts to a modest height seems to say that God's in His heaven and all's right with His world.

—EDITH SHANNON

Historic
Churches
of the
South

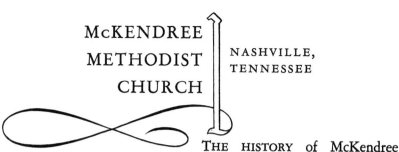

McKENDREE METHODIST CHURCH

NASHVILLE, TENNESSEE

THE HISTORY of McKendree Methodist Church begins with the arrival of the first Methodist circuit rider in Tennessee. Back in 1787, Benjamin Ogden, twenty-three-year-old veteran of the Revolutionary War, came to the village crossroads of Nashville to begin his service as Methodist missionary to the Cumberland Circuit.

He held services in Nashville's courthouse and in private homes in the village and at the other stops on his circuit.

At the end of the year his report described his work in Nashville and ended with the statement that the church had "63 members, four of whom are colored." Wilson Lee followed Mr. Ogden, and it was his privilege to organize the first Society of Methodists in Nashville, to complete the first church building in the city in 1790, and to admit to church membership James Robertson, the founder of Nashville, and his wife, Charlotte.

The site of the first church was deeded to five members of the congregation by an Act of the First Tennessee Legislature which met in Knoxville in March, 1796. It was an important church and many of the early leaders of Methodism in the South preached in it.

The building was soon removed to make way for business houses and dwellings which bordered the public square. For five years the Methodists worshipped in the county jail, an arrangement which had obvious disadvantages. Then, in 1812, the church erected a building on Broad Street. The State Legislature was allowed to use it as a meeting place during the three sessions of 1812-1815. This church was soon too small and in 1817 the congregation built a 63 ...

One of the great churches of Methodism, McKendree Methodist Church has been a vital factor in the religious life of Nashville for 164 years.

large church on Spring Street on land given by George Poyser. This building covered the whole lot and the auditorium had galleries in the rear and on both sides. In 1818 it became a station and the pastor, John Johnson, received all of $232 and table expenses for the year's work to "care for his family of a wife and two children."

In March 1832, the church purchased the site on which it now stands. The new building was completed in 1833 and was dedicated by Bishop William McKendree, for whom it was named. The Bishop preached in this church many times, and it was here on November 23, 1834, that he preached his last sermon, sitting in a chair because he was too feeble to stand.

The second church on this site was dedicated on January 29, 1879. This building was known as the "high steeple church" and the congregation was exceedingly proud of it. When it burned on

October 26, 1879, they erected a third church, modeled after it. Bishop Payne dedicated this church May 7, 1882. But McKendree seemed doomed, for this church, too, burned on July 4, 1905.

The congregation tried to move from the location but the Conference would not approve the sale of the property. So they rebuilt. The cornerstone of the fourth structure was laid on November 9, 1907, and the first service in the new building was held on January 16, 1910.

McKendree Church is rich in its missionary traditions. Vanderbilt University, the Methodist Publishing House and many congregations in the city have been largely founded and fostered by her. Scores of missionaries have gone from the church to all parts of the world. Bishop W. R. Lambuth, famous Methodist missionary in China, was once the assistant pastor of this church.

McKendree holds a peculiar interest for the women of Southern Methodism, since it was here that the Woman's Home and Foreign Bible Missions, predecessor of the Woman's Missionary Society, was organized in 1873 by Mrs. Martha Lavinia Kelley.

As far back as the entrance of Colonel Jimmy Jones into the executive office of the state, McKendree was the scene of the inauguration of the governor. Aaron V. Brown, Neal Brown, William B. Campbell and William Trousdale were all inaugurated here. Andrew Johnson, inaugurated in 1835, was the last governor to take the oath of office in the church. Johnson's second inaugural was held in the new State House.

Throughout its 164 years, McKendree has been one of the great churches of Methodism. Five men who served as its pastor were later elevated to the office of bishop. Others served from time to time as leaders in Sunday school work and young people's activities.

The membership today numbers 1,775 and, under the leadership of Dr. Joseph King Vivion, who has served as pastor since 1935, is stronger and more dynamic than it has ever been. In spite of the special difficulties facing the downtown church in a large city and the current trend toward moving churches to the suburbs, the lay leadership of McKendree is persuaded that their church has a definite service to render to the city and will be as useful to this, and future, generations as to those of earlier days.

Historic
Churches
of the
South

SAN JOSÉ MISSION

SAN ANTONIO, TEXAS

SAN ANTONIO'S venerable Mission San José y San Miguel de Aguayo, dating from 1720, has a story filled with romance, legend, and historic significance. It was named in honor of Saint Joseph and in deference to the Marquis of San Miguel de Aguayo, the governor of the Spanish province of Texas. Here, in the years of the mission's greatest prosperity, the patient, toiling Franciscans taught the Indians the crafts of those early days, as well as reading, writing, art and music.

During the era of the Spanish Cross and Sword in the Southwest, San José was described by visitors as the "Queen of the Missions." It was one of four missions in the vicinity of San Antonio, in addition to the famous Alamo which was originally used as a mission. And it was the most beautiful and the most heavily fortified mission in the chain which at one time stretched from East Texas to the Pacific Coast.

As the years passed and the missions were secularized, San José passed into the hands of one religious order after another. It was not until 1931 that its founders, the Franciscans, returned.

The impressive sculpture that adorns the church is the work of Pedro Huizar, the Spanish sculptor who came to New Spain in the late 1720's as the mission's architect and artist. His work has seldom been equaled. According to legend, he executed and named the Rose Window for Rosa Monterrey, the sweetheart he left in Spain. This window and the exquisite facade are his monument, for after they were completed he operated the mission's granary until his death and he is buried nearby.

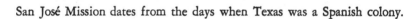
San José Mission dates from the days when Texas was a Spanish colony.

...68

The mission was restored under the direction of Harvey P. Smith, an expert in early Southwestern architecture. Ernest Lenarduzzi, a nationally known sculptor, restored the ornaments and statues of the facade. In 1941, San José was designated a national historic site. It is located about seven miles from the Alamo on highway 287, and is open to visitors the year round, with the exception of the hours of ten to six on Sunday.

The most beautiful and most heavily fortified of the missions in the Southwest, San José was generally known as "the Queen of the Missions."

OLD STONE PRESBYTERIAN CHURCH

LEWISBURG, WEST VIRGINIA

Historic Churches of the South

IF ONE of the hardy pioneers who lived in the Lewisburg area some 150 years ago should come back to the picturesque county seat of Greenbrier County, he would be amazed by the paved streets, the neon signs and the parking meters on the curb—but if he kept on going until he came to Old Stone Presbyterian Church, he would feel right at home. True, he would find the front door where the back door used to be, for the interior was reversed many years ago. And he would marvel at the pipe organ and the electric lights, but otherwise he would find things much the same both inside and outside the building.

Before Old Stone Presbyterian Church was founded in 1783, the word of God was brought to the Greenbrier region by missionaries who tramped the mountain trails, the Bible in one hand, a rifle in the other. When the Reverend John McCue organized the church, it became the first Presbyterian church established west of the Allegheny Mountains. The present structure—the organization's second house of worship—was built in 1796 and is the oldest Protestant church building west of the Alleghenies that has been in continuous use and has not been restored.

The newly organized church soon erected, at a short distance from the little town, a building of unhewn logs covered with clapboards. In the winter, log fires were built in the front yard, but there was no provision, other than the preacher's message, for warming the members of the congregation as they sat inside the building. They would listen to one of the hour-long prayers common in those days, go outside to get warm, then go back inside

Old Stone Presbyterian Church, built in 1796, is the oldest Protestant church building west of the Alleghenies unrestored and in continuous use.

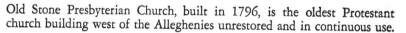
and settle down for another chilly period of spiritual admonition.

Eventually this crude structure was destroyed by fire, and for a time the prospects of building a new one looked pretty dim. The little church had only four elders and 20 members, and while land was abundant, money was scarce.

The congregation was about ready to abandon the project when two of its most loyal members, Colonel and Mrs. John Stuart, offered to furnish the money for the building. Mrs. Stuart had just received a gift of 500 pounds sterling from her father, and her first thought was to give it to the church. Colonel Stuart added 150 pounds from his own pocket, and other members of the congregation made small contributions. The Stuarts also provided a building site, and under the Colonel's direction, construction of the new church was begun.

Stone masons from nearby towns were employed to do the 71 ...

work. And to make the mortar, the women of the congregation carried sand in saddlebags from the Greenbrier River, about four miles away.

Colonel Stuart polished off one of the building stones and inscribed on it: "This building was erected in the year 1796 at the expence (sic) of a few of the first inhabitants of this land to commemorate their affection and esteem for the Holy Gospel of Jesus Christ. Reader, if you are inclined to applaud their virtues, give God the glory." It is significant that, although the Stuarts contributed practically all the funds, they are not mentioned by name in the inscription.

The stone was placed on the front of the building, directly above the door. In later years, when the interior was reversed, the stone was moved to the western end, where churchgoers today may read it as they pass through the door.

In 1830, the small congregation, still made up of only 20 members, decided to enlarge the building, and a pulpit and three Sunday school rooms were added. No addition has been made to the main building since that time. However, at present the approximately 1,100 members of Old Stone are engaged in a major undertaking—the erection of the Old Stone Church religious education building, which will cost about $170,000.

Any account of Old Stone Church would be incomplete without at least a brief mention of the Reverend John McElhenney, who came to it as pastor in 1808. For 62 years this man of God served the church, and such was his hold on the congregation that tradition says some of them walked 20 miles to hear him preach.

The present pastor, the Reverend Dr. Lloyd M. Courtney, has served the church since 1923.

Each Sunday Old Stone's chimes call worshippers to this historic church where time seems to stand still. As an aged sexton once said, "Jest keep it kivered, and it'll last 'til Jedgment Day."

—J. W. BENJAMIN

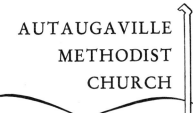

AUTAUGAVILLE METHODIST CHURCH

AUTAUGAVILLE, ALABAMA

AUTAUGAVILLE Methodist Church, formerly known as Asbury Church, has a history that goes back almost to Alabama's beginnings as a state, for the original building was erected in 1822 on the site of "Econachaca," an old Indian village commonly known to the settlers as "Holy Ground." The church was named in honor of Francis Asbury, famous circuit-riding bishop of early American Methodism.

Several years before, in 1814, Andrew Jackson had negotiated a treaty with the Creek Indians whereby they relinquished to the United States their claim to the territory around this part of the Alabama River. Soon afterward, white settlers—among them many religious people, with the Methodists outnumbering the other denominations—began moving into Central Alabama in great numbers. In 1818, some of them settled in the area known as Autauga, an Indian term meaning the "land of plenty." That same year Autauga was made a county, and a year later the Alabama Territory was admitted to the Union as a state.

Also in 1818, the Reverend Alexander Talley was appointed by the South Carolina Conference as a missionary to the Alabama Territory. Arriving on horseback, he settled in the Autaugaville community and established headquarters for his missionary activity. By the end of 1819, Mr. Talley "located"; that is, he ceased to be an itinerant preacher and took up the study and practice of medicine. He continued, however, as a powerful "local" preacher.

Many great camp meetings were held in Autauga in 1819 and 1820, and countless interesting stories have come out of the revi-

Historic Churches of the South

Members of Autaugaville Methodist Church are proud of their "evergreen" Sunday school, which has never closed since it was organized in 1825.

valism of this period. Some people were "gloriously converted" at the camp meetings; others under the "conviction of sin" were later converted in their homes; and still others came to salvation riding or walking along the roads as they returned home from the meetings. All of this religious fervor led to the firm establishment of a church which has continued through the years in uninterrupted service to the Autaugaville community.

In 1822, the first Asbury Church building was erected, but in a few years this log cabin church began to fall apart. A larger, more comfortable frame structure was built, and Asbury Church prospered.

Prominent in the history of Central Alabama and Autaugaville Methodism were Seaborn Mims and his wife, who operated an inn at which many travelers stopped for meals and overnight lodging. In the fall of 1825, there stopped at the inn a traveler whose distinguished bearing attracted the notice of all the other guests. They were reluctant to question him, and he did not volunteer any information about himself. Mr. and Mrs. Mims, however, extended him the hospitality of the inn and invited him to attend religious services with them at Asbury Church. There, everyone noticed that he entered into the services with a great deal of feeling.

Upon their return to the inn, this handsome stranger asked if he might read a passage of Scripture and have family prayer with the innkeepers and their guests. After he had conducted the brief service, he was accompanied to his room by some of the men and questioned as to his identity and purpose. He was Bishop Robert H. Roberts, and he had come to Autaugaville to encourage the church. He said he was jubilant to find it so "staunch and deep-dyed in Christianity."

As one of the guests put it, "By entertaining a stranger, we had the honor of entertaining a live bishop unawares!"

In 1829, a group of members pulled away from Asbury Church and organized a new church, erecting a building in Smedley

Grove. But in 1867, there was a reunion of Smedley Grove and Asbury, and Methodism in Autaugaville found itself strengthened and revitalized. The old Smedley Grove building was rolled from its original location to its present site, where it serves today as the Autaugaville Methodist Church.

Relics of the old days have been put to modern use in the Autaugaville Church. The slave gallery is used as a meeting place for a Sunday school class, and the old oil-lamp chandelier is equipped with electric bulbs.

Since its organization in 1822, the church has never been without a preacher, and old-timers speak with pride of their "evergreen" Sunday school, which was organized in 1825 and which has never closed through all the long history of the church.

—ROBERT H. WALSTON

VINE STREET CHRISTIAN CHURCH

NASHVILLE, TENNESSEE

THE HISTORY OF Vine Street Christian Church is one of the most eventful to be found in Southern religious annals. It was, at the outset, a Baptist church on Spring Street (now Church Street). The Spring Street body started in 1820 as the first Baptist congregation in Nashville, which then had a population of only 4,000. The church was described as a "large, well-arranged frame building, one of the finest houses of worship in the city," and it cost every bit of $6,000.

The thriving young Baptist church called to its pulpit Philip Fall, a youthful Englishman. Fall, whose ideas of religion didn't exactly jibe with the traditional concepts of the church, soon converted his congregation to his own beliefs.

The young minister later fell under the spell of Alexander Campbell—one of the founders of the Disciples of Christ movement—and in 1827, a year after Fall became pastor of the church, Campbell visited Nashville. The force of Campbell's preaching and Fall's influence led the Spring Street congregation to withdraw from the Concord Baptist Association. The following year it voted to reorganize "in full sympathy with the reform principles of Alexander Campbell," and Philip Fall became popularly known as "the father of the Christian Church in the South."

When the Spring Street congregation voted itself away from the Baptist Church, only five members stuck to their original faith. For the time being, this almost ruined the Baptist movement in Nashville. But the five remaining Baptists, with a few newcomers, started another church which later became the First Baptist Church, 77 ...

Historic Churches of the South

One of the early storm centers of the Disciples of Christ movement, Vine Street Christian Church has had a remarkably eventful history.

now one of the city's largest congregations, and today the Baptists make up one of the largest religious groups in Nashville.

Under Fall's pastorship and Campbell's influence, the Spring Street Church became one of the early storm centers of the whole Disciples movement. The building rang with violent debates, for these were the days when devout opponents met in scriptural combat and championed their interpretation of Divine will with hours of religious argument and oratorical pyrotechnics.

Fall's first ministry ended in 1831, when he left for 27 years of teaching and other work in Kentucky. He returned in 1858 to serve as pastor until his retirement in 1876.

During Fall's 27-year absence from the Spring Street Church, the pulpit was occupied for a nine-year period (1847-1856) by
Jesse Ferguson, a dynamic young preacher whose popularity

proved phenomenal. He overflowed his church with every class of people from tramps and gamblers to society's upper crust, somewhat to the dismay of the latter. Under his driving power a handsome new $30,000 building was erected on Cherry Street.

Ferguson, however, developed a strong belief in spiritualism and indulged in seances, table-knocking, spirit-rapping and every sort of necromancy. He converted some of his congregation to his belief in mysticism and Alexander Campbell, alarmed by this turn of events, hurried back to Nashville to help straighten things out. In 1856, many members pulled out and returned to the original Spring Street building. A year later, the fine new Cherry Street structure burned to the ground, and the Ferguson faction died out.

During the War Between the States, the Spring Street congregation, with Mr. Fall as pastor, didn't suffer quite as many indignities under Federal troop occupation as did the other Nashville churches. Most of the city's pastors were imprisoned for their Confederate allegiance and their churches were closed. Fall, however, took refuge in his status as an English citizen and rather dared the Yankees to do anything about it, although his sons were fighting under the Confederate banner. His church remained open.

The congregation remained at the Spring Street location until they moved to the present building on Seventh Avenue, which was then Vine Street. This building, known today as Vine Street Christian Church, was completed in 1889. In its 63 years at the present site, the church has had eight pastors. Two of the best loved ministers were its two most recent, Dr. Carey Morgan and Dr. Roger T. Nooe, whose combined ministries totaled nearly 40 years. Dr. Nooe recently retired to be succeeded by Dr. G. Curtis Jones, one of the Disciples' most popular ministers.

The present church body has a membership of 1,500. It maintains a home for elderly women in Nashville, and supports a missionary and missionary nurse in India. It has also founded and helped to finance two branch churches in Nashville.

—Ross L. Holman   79...

THE CHURCH IN THE WILDWOOD

LEON COUNTY, FLORIDA

IN A VIRGIN FOREST of moss-draped live oaks, hickory, pine and magnolias eleven miles northeast of Tallahassee, stands Pisgah Church, the oldest Methodist church in Florida. This modest frame building, the third to be erected on the original site, is in the center of a rich agricultural area, known from pioneer times as the Centerville community. Both community and church are fringed by a chain of lakes—Iamonia, Jackson, Miccosukee and Lafayette—which were the hunting and fishing grounds of the hostile Mikasuke and Seminole Indians at the time Pisgah Church was established.

Although time has brought about many changes, and the membership of Pisgah—like that of many rural churches—has decreased through the years, services are held here once a month. And once a year on the first Sunday in May, when the surrounding countryside is at its loveliest, there is an all-day homecoming service. At this time, church dignitaries from all over the state and friends and descendants of Pisgah pioneer parishioners make a pilgrimage to the little white church in the lonely grove "to worship God in the beauty of holiness," to meet old friends and to share a picnic lunch.

The church body is far older than the wooden structure that is now its home. Pisgah Church dates back to early territorial days, immediately following the transfer of Florida from Spain to the United States on February 22, 1819. The Territory of Florida was created and civil government established by the Congressional Act of March 30, 1822. But even in 1820, before the Stars and Stripes

Pisgah, the "Church in the Wildwood," was founded in the days of the Territory of Florida and is the oldest Methodist church in the state.

replaced the Spanish flag, colonists from Virginia and the Carolinas, attracted by the fertile soil of the rolling, red clay hill country, had laid out their plantations in the Centerville community. And by the time they had built their homes and planted their crops, they already had plans underway for a place of worship.

The site they selected was called Pisgah. According to old settlers, the first services at Pisgah were held under a brush arbor, and soon thereafter in a log cabin of hand-hewn pine poles. The men of the community sawed out a door, hewed puncheons for floor and seats, made a rude table, and considered the building complete.

Since church records were not kept prior to 1830, the exact date of the completion of this first church building is not known; however, according to early writers on Methodism in Florida, such pioneer circuit riders as John Triggs and John Slade, who was often called "the father of Methodism in Florida," occasionally preached there during the early 1820's.

The Pisgah organization, insofar as provision for a pastor is concerned, had its beginning in 1825 with the creation of a new Methodist district with headquarters in Tallahassee. The Pisgah charge was included in this district.

In the first few years of the church's existence, progress was slow and life was difficult for these sturdy, God-fearing pioneers. There were no roads. Circuit riders and many members rode to church over rough, narrow Indian trails, while others walked several miles through the woods. The men kept their muskets at hand during church services, and some of them remained outside the building to protect worshippers from possible sneak attack by Seminole Indians from nearby Lake Lafayette.

As the population of the community increased, a sawmill moved in. Then roads were built and, finally, a new frame church was erected.

The next few years were especially trying ones for Pisgah communicants. In his *History of Methodism in Georgia and Florida,* George G. Smith says that during 1837-38 there was a call for the highest heroism on the part of everyone. "The cruel and unconquerable Seminoles were waging an exterminating war with torch, tomahawk and rifle, and the preachers of this section held their own at the risk of their lives," he writes. Not all escaped with their lives. Several were shot from their horses and killed while en route to their appointments. And among their congregations, whole families were massacred.

At the close of the Seminole Wars in 1842, Pisgah began to take on new life. From 1845 until the outbreak of the War Between the States, the church apparently was quite prosperous, as was the community, which had developed a thriving ante-bellum cotton and tobacco aristocracy.

In 1858, the Reverend Robert H. Howren, a distinguished Methodist of that day, assumed the pastorate of Pisgah. Mr. Howren had

performed heroic service during the Seminole Wars, ministering to the spiritual and physical needs of soldiers as well as those of the terrorized citizens sheltered in the churches and blockhouses. While at Pisgah, he made plans and raised sufficient funds for the present church building, which was dedicated in 1859.

The Reverend Simon Peter Richardson, another outstanding Methodist leader who served Pisgah before and during the War Between the States, says in his *Lights and Shadows of Itinerant Life,* "There were fine people in this heavily populated community, people of refinement and wealth, and there was not a man, woman or child at Pisgah old enough to join the church that was left out." It was during the Reverend Mr. Richardson's pastorate that a parsonage and academy were built at Pisgah; however, these have long since disappeared.

Mr. Richardson was a strict disciplinarian, as well as a great preacher. A well-known Georgia newspaperman tells of a conversation that he once had with the famous clergyman. On the minister's return from a meeting, the journalist inquired, "What kind of a meeting did you have today, Uncle Simon?"

"Oh, we had a glorious meeting!" was the reply.

"How many members did you take in?"

"Not a single one," the minister said, "but we turned out seventeen and purged the church. Oh, but it was a glorious meeting!"

When the War Between the States broke out, the Pisgah congregation rallied to the Southern cause and several of its physician members served as Confederate Army surgeons. The church was frequently the meeting place of the old men of the community, who were organized into a home defense unit known as the "Old Guards." They were led by their pastor and captain, the Reverend Mr. Richardson.

But despite those trying times and postwar reconstruction days, and the general exodus to the cities that followed, there has not been a break in the services at Pisgah since 1830.

Pisgah is one of the churches featured on the "Tallahassee Trail" during the last week in February, when historic homes and churches of the vicinity are opened to the public.

As the visitor enters the church, his attention is drawn immediately to the classically beautiful white chancel and the old slave balcony. One of the exhibits of greatest interest is the collection of miniature models of places of worship at Pisgah. These are exact replicas, complete in every detail. Even the brush arbor is represented. There is also an old Communion service of heavy silver, which has been preserved in the homes of the remaining members. Other treasured items are some very old Bibles, a 100-year-old square piano, and a collection of hymnals without notes for "Publick, Social and Domestic Worship."

Today Pisgah Church has fewer than fifty members, and they find it difficult to carry on the work of the church and keep the building from falling into disrepair. But they are determined that Pisgah will continue to play its role in the life of the community. As one member expresses it, "Our forebears left us a rich heritage, and the work of Pisgah will go on."

—BLANCHE SYFRET MCKNIGHT

Historic Churches of the South

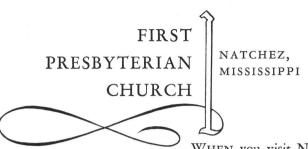

FIRST PRESBYTERIAN CHURCH

NATCHEZ, MISSISSIPPI

WHEN you visit Natchez, make it a point to see some of the historic churches as well as the old homes for which this romantic river town is famous. One of the most impressive is the First Presbyterian Church. It is interesting not only because of its age and its history, but for its architectural excellence and the faithful preservation of its interior.

Entering its massive paneled doors, you will find quaint old cushioned wooden pews with button-latched gates. The light from the handsome arched windows falls gently on red carpeting, white woodwork and soft blue-gray walls. The old slave gallery is still there to complete the picture of ante-bellum days.

But this church is more than a monument to the splendor of the Old South; it is a vigorous church, alert to the needs of the present and full of plans for the future. Accommodations for the church school and various other phases of present-day religious activity have been added at the rear of the main auditorium, but in such a way that they do not detract from the architectural beauty of the building proper.

The First Presbyterian Church has been in existence since leaders of the congregation purchased the building site on February 20, 1812. Even before that date there was a Presbyterian organization in the Natchez country, for home missionaries came to the region as early as 1799.

The first church building was started in 1812 but was not completed until 1817 because the financial panic which swept the country in 1812 made the raising of funds almost impossible. 85 ...

Stately First Presbyterian Church is one of the showplaces of Natchez.

When the structure was completed in 1817, the Reverend Daniel Smith became the church's first pastor.

At that time Natchez was the capital of Mississippi and a thriving river port. The church building soon became too small for its congregation, and in 1828 it was razed to make room for a larger and handsomer house of worship. The lot was lowered and the present building erected on the old site. The church building which you see today was dedicated on January 1, 1830.

Eleven regular pastors have served this church since 1820. One served the church for 60 years; Dr. Joseph B. Stratton began his ministry in November, 1843, and remained until April 14, 1894, when he became pastor emeritus, in which capacity he served until October 1903.

Historic Churches of the South

Many changes occurred during Dr. Stratton's pastorate. During the years of Natchez' commercial prosperity he watched the building of the fine plantation and town houses. When the War Between the States broke out, the members of his church rallied to the Southern cause. During the war the church helped shelter the homeless, feed the hungry, and served as both a spiritual and physical sanctuary. Natchez was shelled by Commodore Porter and Federal troops occupied the city in 1863. The damages to the church structure were easily repaired, but the early days of postwar reconstruction were trying times. Fortunes had disappeared and with them the old way of life. The church managed to survive, and the years since have been more placid ones. In 1929, the church held its centenary celebration. Today it is able to review its past with pride and to look confidently toward the future.

CHRIST CHURCH

SAVANNAH, GEORGIA

Historic **C**hurches *of the* **S**outh

NEARLY fifty years before Robert Raikes started that much-disputed "world's first Sunday school," John Wesley, minister of Christ Church in Savannah, Georgia, had already established classes for religious instruction of children. Except for a short time during the American Revolution, this Sunday school has been functioning ever since.

Organized according to directions given to General James Edward Oglethorpe by the Trustees of the Colony of Georgia, Christ Episcopal Church was closely associated with the early history of Georgia and the development of Savannah. Christ Church parish covered a wide territory, extending from the Savannah River to the Great Ogeechee, and from halfway to Augusta, in the northern part of the colony, down to Tybee lighthouse, where the Savannah River joins the Atlantic Ocean.

For the first few years after the founding of the Colony of Georgia, church services were held in the open air, in General Oglethorpe's tent, in the Court House, and finally in the first church building on the present site facing Johnson Square on Bull Street. The first silver Communion service for the church was a gift from Samuel Wesley, father of John and Charles Wesley, and the first organ ever brought to Georgia was presented to Christ Church, in 1766, by Colonel Barnard of Augusta. The church bell was made by Paul Revere, of Revolutionary War fame.

The oldest church in the State of Georgia and one of the oldest in this country, Christ Church has been associated with notable events and persons in the growth of Savannah since 1733. It was

Historic Churches of the South

One of the oldest churches in the United States, Christ Church has been closely associated with notable names and events in Savannah since 1733.

in Savannah that John Wesley, while minister at Christ Church, had that unhappy love affair that changed his whole life, sending him out into the world to become one of the great religious leaders of the ages. It was in Savannah, during his ministry at Christ Church, that John Wesley wrote the first book written in Georgia and the first hymnal of the Church of England—the *Charlestown Collection of Psalms and Hymns,* printed in Charleston, South Carolina, in 1737, because the four-year-old colony across the river did not have the necessary equipment. Wesley also conducted one of this country's earliest circulating libraries while he was rector at Christ Church.

Succeeding Wesley as minister at Christ Church was the young George Whitefield, responsible for the building, in 1740, of the first home for the orphan children of the new colony. Named Bethesda, "House of Mercy," this orphanage was built on a 500-acre tract of land granted by the King of England.

Among the distinguished persons associated with the church in

Juliette Low, founder of the Girl Scouts, worshipped in this church.

the present century was Juliette Low, founder of the Girl Scouts. To this organization, the steps of Christ Church have a particular significance. It was there that Mrs. Low stopped her cousin, Mrs. J. Randolph Anderson, after services on a Sunday in 1912 and told her of her plan to start the Girl Guides in this country. She asked Mrs. Anderson to serve as the first captain, and young Page Anderson and her little friends made up the first troop. Thus the first Girl Scout troop, the "White Rose" troop, had its beginning.

Fifteen years later, Girl Scouts of Savannah were the honorary escort at the funeral of Juliette Low. They stood at attention on the steps of Christ Church as the body of their leader was borne into the church.

Dedicated in 1751, the first building of Christ Church was destroyed by fire in 1796. A new building was constructed in 1803, damaged by storm in 1804, and rebuilt in 1810. The present building was erected in 1838.

Christ Church has memories of many important events that occurred since Oglethorpe laid out "a site for a Church" in 1733. One of the most important concerns John Wesley, the little man in black ministerial robes who taught the children on Sunday afternoon during the early days of the church's history.

—MARGARET GODLEY

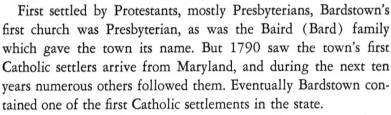

ST. JOSEPH'S PROTO-CATHEDRAL

BARDSTOWN, KENTUCKY

THE STORY of St. Joseph's Cathedral of Bardstown is the story of the men who established the Roman Catholic faith in Kentucky.

First settled by Protestants, mostly Presbyterians, Bardstown's first church was Presbyterian, as was the Baird (Bard) family which gave the town its name. But 1790 saw the town's first Catholic settlers arrive from Maryland, and during the next ten years numerous others followed them. Eventually Bardstown contained one of the first Catholic settlements in the state.

About the turn of the century, St. Joseph's Church was built. It was only a log chapel and, as so often happened with these pioneer churches, the growth of the membership quickly exceeded the expectations of the builders, space proved inadequate, and private homes had to be used as meeting places.

Father Whelan, an Irish Franciscan, served as missionary to the first few Bardstown faithful. He was succeeded in 1789 by Father William de Rohan, and Father Stephen Theodore Badin followed in 1793.

Even among the heroic figures who peopled Kentucky's history during this period, Father Badin was outstanding. For seven years he was the only priest in the Commonwealth of Kentucky. He was born and educated in France, but fled to America during the Revolution, and was thus the first priest to be ordained in this country. He has been aptly named the Patriarch of Catholicity in Kentucky. His journeys on horseback totaled oven ten thousand miles. He continually suffered all the hardships of that perilous time, often lacking the bare necessities of life.

St. Joseph's Proto-Cathedral is filled with art treasures which, according to local legend, were a gift from King Louis Philippe of France.

He was not one, however, to allow the austerity of such a life to rob him of his sense of humor. It has been said that Father Badin's quick wit and great personal charm did much to overcome the prejudice of the early settlers against the Catholic Church. Typical of the many stories told about him is the one which relates how a Presbyterian minister met him afoot on the road between Bardstown and Fairfield.

"Father Badin, where is your horse?" was the immediate question.

"He was taken sick and died on the road," the priest replied.

"And did you give him absolution before he died?"

"That would have been useless," said the priest, with a twinkle in his eye. "The poor animal turned Presbyterian in his dying moments and went straight to hell!"

Father Badin was later to be joined in Kentucky by three other priests, and welcome they must have been. One was Charles Nerinckx, a Belgian, whom many credit with being the equal of Badin in physical and intellectual zeal. On his arrival in 1805, he first took up residence with Badin in a rough log cabin at St. Stephen's, now the Loretto Motherhouse. The next year he moved to a farm four miles from Bardstown, a gift to the church from one Thomas Howard. When a seminary was opened there, the donor was remembered in its name, St. Thomas. Placed in charge here was Father John Baptist David, who had joined Badin in his flight from France.

About this time, Bishop Carroll of Baltimore petitioned Rome for help in caring for his rapidly multiplying flock in the New World. His request was granted. Four new sees were formed—New York, Boston, Philadelphia and Bardstown. Appointed to serve as bishop of the new see of Bardstown was another young French refugee priest, Father Benedict Flaget. Traditionally, he was not easily persuaded to accept the post, feeling himself too humble for either the responsibility or the honor entailed. But eventually he arrived in Bardstown, where he was to be the spiritual head of some 1,000 Catholic families, ministered to by ten churches or chapels. Six other churches were under construction.

Flaget's humility was apparently no handicap in the performance of his duties as bishop. Soon he was planning and working to raise funds for the construction of "his Cathedral." By 1816, he was able to write the following letter to the Bishop of Quebec:

"Poor though I be, my aspirations are high, for in a few weeks I am going to Bardstown with all the ecclesiastics I can gather, there to lay the cornerstone of my Cathedral. It is to be 120 feet long, 30 feet in the sanctuary, 90 in the nave, and 65 feet in width. The foundations are of stone, resting on rock; the remainder will be brick. The style is chiefly Corinthian.

"The builder, John Rogers, who is very able and a good Catholic, believes it will cost between $15,000 and $20,000, a prodigious sum which assuredly will not be found in the treasury of the Bishop of Bardstown, but rather in the inexhaustible riches of Divine Providence.

". . . I trust you, Monsignor, . . . will procure for me whatever assistance you can in erecting this monument, the first of its kind in this vast territory. They (the Bardstown townspeople) have subscribed almost entirely among themselves nearly $10,000. I hope to get $4,000 or $5,000 more in the country, but the remainder must come from well disposed and charitable persons of other places."

Even the $10,000 already collected was a "prodigious sum" in those uninflated times. John Rogers, the architect who had drawn the plans for the imposing structure, moved from Baltimore to Bardstown to superintend the erection. The cathedral, with its six massive columns, shows the strong classical influence reflected in Southern architecture at the time, and only a few minor changes have been made in the building since its construction.

With almost no exceptions, native Kentucky building materials 95 . . .

were used in the cathedral. A local limestone quarry furnished the stone for the foundation, and the red brick was burned in a yard nearby, using the native clays. The nails and hardware were wrought by Bardstown blacksmiths. From the surrounding forest came the fine woods used in the interior of the building, as well as the six enormous poplar trees, which were hauled in by oxen to form the great pillars.

Everything could be had in abundance, it seemed, except money. It was three years before the cathedral was dedicated, and more than once during that time construction came to a standstill for want of funds. In one of his letters, Father Nerinckx relates how he returned from a trip abroad to find the cathedral nearing completion, but all work halted by financial difficulties. Nerinckx had brought with him a beautiful mechanical clock from Flanders, but since the steeple of the building was not yet begun, John Rogers mounted the clock in the front wall. The townspeople listened, entranced, as its two little silver-toned bells struck the hours. Such a clock, public sentiment agreed, deserved a steeple. Almost overnight enough money was raised to complete the cathedral, including a steeple for the precious clock.

Badin, Nerinckx and Flaget were responsible for securing nearly all of the numerous paintings and art treasures which are to be found within the cathedral today. From each of their trips to Europe they returned with precious gifts, many of them relics from churches of France and Belgium, burned and pillaged during the Napoleonic era. Murillo, Rubens, van Dyck, Jacob Hast and others are represented here.

Legend has it that most of these treasures come from another—and more romantic—source: The tale begins in Havana, Cuba. Louis Philippe, Duke of Orleans, as yet only an impoverished exile from France, was befriended by another exile, Father Flaget, then an equally poor priest. Years later, the royal wanderer appeared in Bardstown, where he was again befriended by the same man, then a bishop busy with the construction of his fine new cathedral. Bardstown folk maintain that Louis Philippe lived in their town for several years, took the name of Smith, and eked out a less than royal living by repairing watches and giving French and dancing lessons.

Then Louis Philippe was recalled by France and became her king, and through the years that followed his gratitude to Flaget took the form of fabulous gifts which were to glorify St. Joseph's Cathedral: magnificent religious paintings, the cathedral bell, and—embroidered by his queen and her maids—the gorgeous vestments which can be seen today.

Small wonder the legend has persisted so tenaciously. It is a pretty tale and, moreover, a moral one. Princes are seldom so noted for their gratitude, nor do they often show it in such spectacular fashion. One would like to believe it true, but it would seem a pity so to depreciate the work done by pioneer priests and the generosity of the true donors in thus furnishing their cathedral. Actually, there is little evidence that Louis Philippe spent more than few hours in Bardstown, simply passing through on his way from Tennessee to Ohio.

In 1841, the episcopal see was moved to Louisville, where a new cathedral was built. From that time on, St. Joseph's was known as the Proto (or first) Cathedral.

Today St. Joseph's Proto-Cathedral attracts visitors of every faith from all over the world. Whether they look upon its art treasures as tokens of royal gratitude or as symbols of priestly labor and self-sacrifice, they find a visit within its walls an inspiring experience.

—SUE McCLELLAND THIERMAN

ST. PETER'S CHURCH

ST. PETER'S CHURCH was built 249 years ago on a knoll not far from the York River in New Kent County, Virginia. During the colonial period it was intimately related to the life of its parishioners, since the Church of England, by "Their Majesties' order," was the stern regulator of the morals of the people.

Since this church building was the largest "publick building" in the county, meetings were held here when colonial affairs had to be discussed. Copies of all civil notices were posted on its doors. Social affairs revolved about the church, and communicants enjoyed their "social hour" in the churchyard after Sunday services were over.

Many of the famous first families of Virginia were communicants at St. Peter's. Col. John Dandridge and his family were members, as were the Custis family who lived at White Hall plantation, near the Pamunkey River. It is said that James Blair, founder of William and Mary College and, for many years, acting governor of the colony, preached at St. Peter's on several occasions.

But life did not always run smoothly in the parish. One of the early ministers, the Reverend Nicholas Moreau, wrote to the Bishop of London soon after he arrived. "I have got into the very worst parish in Virginia and most troublesome." Later he wrote again, this time to plead with the same bishop that the Church of England should appoint a Bishop of Virginia whose duties would be "to make hell tremble and to settle the Church of England here forever." In the years that followed, however, many changes occurred,

St. Peter's Church, which was built 249 years ago, has acquired fame as the place where George Washington and Martha Custis were *not* married.

for rectors who followed the Reverend Mr. Moreau found the parish most desirable. *89209*

Construction of the church building began in 1701, but it was not opened for services until two years later. Funds for building the church were obtained, so legend tells us, by levying a tax on every pound of tobacco raised in the county during those years. A heavy tower, broken by three arched openings, protected the entrance and gave the church the Tudor design so popular in England at this time. One Will Hughes, architect and builder, drew up the plans and built the structure under the supervision of the vestry. Severely plain rectangular windows were used, and the interior was almost austere in its simplicity.

The church was the scene of many of the meetings held before the Revolutionary War. During the war women and children used the church as a refuge from the British.

During the War Between the States the church was used as a stable by Federal troops. Soldiers carved their names on the walls of the entrance; some of them are legible to this day. Extensive repairs were made after the war ended, and since that time only maintenance repairs have been necessary.

The most famous rector of St. Peter's, the Reverend David Mossom, was a man of fiery temperament, given to heated argument. In Bishop Meade's famous book on Virginia families and churches he mentions Mr. Mossom. "He was married four times and much harrassed by his last wife, as Colonel Basset has often told me, which may account for and somewhat excuse a little peevishness." Evidently the parishioners were sympathetic, for he served as rector from 1727 to 1767. He was the first American admitted to the office of presbyter in the Church of England.

The church has acquired fame as the place where George Washington and Martha Custis were *not* married. The Reverend Mr. Mossom performed the ceremony for the famous couple on January 6, 1759, but the wedding (one of the most brilliant ever solemnized in Virginia) took place at White Hall, the Custis plantation. It is only natural that many people have assumed that the wedding took place in the little church, for Martha Dandridge Custis was christened here, and was a regular communicant at St. Peter's for almost half her life.

Today, services are held in St. Peter's Church, now Protestant Episcopal, on one Sunday each month.

Visitors often stop to see this venerable structure as they drive from Richmond to Williamsburg. Sir Francis Bacon's remark, "It is a reverend thing to see an ancient castle not in decay," might well be paraphrased to apply to this structure. Noteworthy, too, is the fact that St. Peter's has remained a vital influence through the years in the lives of those who live and have lived in New Kent County, Virginia.

FIRST BAPTIST CHURCH

THE FIRST BAPTIST CHURCH of Augusta, Georgia, with a present membership of over 2,500, adds weight to Tennyson's words, "More things are wrought by prayer than this world dreams of."

Back in the 1730's, Augusta was only a trading post on the Savannah River. A handful of Baptists lived in the settlement, but since the Colony of Georgia was under British dominion, the official church was the Church of England.

It was not until 1817 that the few Baptists in Augusta decided to organize. On March 25 of that year, eight men and ten women met under the leadership of one Jesse Green. Their quaint recorded covenant reads in part: "We, the Baptist brethren of Augusta, Georgia, being in destitute state without preaching, church union or Communion . . . have thought proper to enter into the following covenant, viz: We agree to join in a society to be known and styled The Baptist Praying Society of Augusta . . ."

Two years later they called a pastor, William T. Brantly, a scholarly man who had been a community leader some years earlier and who was returning to Augusta to reassume the post of principal of the Academy of Richmond County, which had been established after the close of the Revoluntionary War. Dr. Brantly accepted the church's call, but refused to accept a salary until a church could be built and paid for.

On January 20, 1820, the church was formally reorganized, and by May a constitution of eighteen articles had been drawn up by Dr. Brantly and adopted "without argument or dissent."

Historic Churches of the South

The First Baptist Church, organized in 1817 as "The Baptist Praying Society of Augusta" with a membership of eighteen, now has 2,500 members.

Dr. Brantly's eloquence and forceful personality soon filled the Academy chapel where the Baptists met for worship.

A church building was the next consideration. The site of the present church was purchased for $1,500 and plans were made for a building to cost $20,000, an ambitious project for a small congregation of that day. But the members gave generously and some wealthy and influential friends of the pastor lent financial assist- ...102 ance. On May 26, 1821, the beautiful new church was dedicated

The Southern Baptist Convention was organized in this church auditorium.

to the worship of God. The text of Dr. Brantly's dedication sermon was "Establish Thou the work of our hands."

In the years that followed, Augusta suffered from floods, fire, and epidemics of cholera and yellow fever, but the congregation grew in size and spiritual influence. During this time the church accepted into membership a young man named William Melton Tryon who was destined to play an important role in Christian education in the South. It was he who later established the first Baptist church in Houston, Texas, and was instrumental in founding Baylor University, the first institute for higher education in Texas.

Years passed, and the church, now known as the First Baptist Church of Augusta, fostered new branches in other sections of the growing city.

The question of slavery had become a fiery issue throughout the country. By 1844, the question had arisen in the church body at large, and serious friction arose in the Triennial Convention, an organization representing missionary enterprises of Baptist churches in both the North and South.

The Baptist Foreign Missionary Board of Virginia issued a call to Baptist churches of the South to send delegates to a convention to meet in Augusta on May 8, 1845, and 327 messengers from the District of Columbia, Virginia, North Carolina, South Carolina, Kentucky, Florida, Alabama, Mississippi, and Georgia, met there to deliberate on the problem that threatened the missionary activities of the South.

For four days the delegates planned and discussed steps they must take. A representative of Virginia read to those assembled a letter written by a noted minister in the North, which casts an interesting light on the attitude of the day.

"You will separate," he wrote. "I could not ask otherwise. Your rights have been infringed. . . . We have shown how Christians ...104 ought not to act; it remains for you to show us how they ought to act. Put away all violence; act with dignity and the world will approve your course."

In this spirit the convention organized The Southern Baptist Convention.

As the church grew, the original building was improved and enlarged, but in 1900 it reached the point where no further expansion was possible and a new one had to be built. The fine new edifice, dedicated with a full week of services beginning December 1, 1903, marked the passage from an old era to the new. More recently an educational building has been added and adjacent land procured, more than doubling in size the original site.

In 1819, two deacons were sufficient for the church's needs. Today, under the leadership of Dr. A. Warren Huyck, 37 deacons, prominent in the business and professional life of Augusta, serve to further the church's usefulness and activities.

The dedicatory text of May 6, 1821, "Establish Thou the work of our hands," has been fulfilled in greater measure, perhaps, than the founding eighteen members dared to dream.

—DOROTHY LEHMAN SUMERAU

Historic Churches of the South

STEELE CREEK PRESBYTERIAN CHURCH

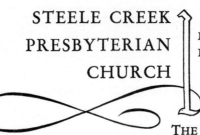

Historic Churches of the South

THE FREEDOM-LOVING, God-fearing Scotch-Irish settlers who pushed into the Carolinas in the 1700's and settled along Steele Creek, probably held their first religious service in an oak grove. These pioneers were more interested in making history than in writing it, and they left no written record of the early days of Steele Creek Presbyterian Church, now the largest rural church in General Assembly of the Presbyterian Church, U. S. A.

Years later, the Reverend John Douglas, who served as pastor from 1866 to 1879, was annoyed by the remark of the North Carolina historian Foote that "Steele Creek has no history," so he painstakingly studied records of New York and Philadelphia synods and gave Steele Creek a written history. He established the founding date as 1760, and learned that in its first few years, Steele Creek Church was served by men sent out by the synods of New York and Philadelphia.

In 1767, the Reverend Robert Henry was secured as the first resident pastor. His labors in the church were brief, however, and there followed a time when the congregation was without a minister. This period included the Revolutionary War years, when the men of Steele Creek took an active part in the rebellion against the mother country. Robert Irwin and Zaccheus Wilson, two of the signers of the Mecklenburg Declaration of Independence (May 20, 1775), were ruling elders from Steele Creek.

Two of the early church buildings were destroyed by fire. The fifth and present one was erected in 1889, and the Sunday school building was added in 1923.

Steele Creek Presbyterian Church, founded in 1760, is the largest rural church in the General Assembly of the Presbyterian Church, U. S. A.

During the years of World War II, members raised a fund for the improvement of the church building, and in 1950 a complete remodeling program was started. In July of that year the congregation moved out of the church and Sunday school buildings into the large, barn-like community house on the grounds. A temporary pulpit and choir loft were erected, and everyone agreed that the emergency arrangements were not bad at all. On January 7, 1951, the first service was held in the "new" church, and every seat was filled.

All that could be left unchanged was untouched in remodeling, for tradition and sentiment are strong in this church. However, a group of windows set in an arch in the center front of the building gave way to a large door; this and the two original doors flanking it open into a vestibule. At each end of the vestibule a stairway leads to the balcony, which is still used as a Sunday school class- 107 . . .

room. The wainscoting and choir loft are of walnut paneling, so the old ceiling beams received a coat of walnut-toned paint. The plastered walls were painted gray.

The community house, which was built in 1926, came in for its share of remodeling. A chapel, seating 100, was built across the front of the house, a Sunday school room and a kitchen across the back.

The Reverend Watt Martin Cooper, Steele Creek's twentieth pastor, has served the church since 1949. Under his leadership Steele Creek has made progress toward more effective organization and has added many new members.

The women of the Steele Creek church have played a prominent part in its growth. The first women's organization was formed in 1880 and was known as The Ladies Benevolent Aid Society. Mr. J. J. Price was chaplain, as women did not pray in public at that time. April 4, 1888, was a milestone in the history of the women of Steele Creek Church, for on that day Miss Maggie Whiteside was persuaded to offer a prayer in the meeting.

There is also a bit of information on good authority that a Steele Creek Female Book Society was organized as early as 1821 with a membership of 104 and a library of 116 volumes. This was not a church project, but the women were members of the church and went there for their meetings.

Steele Creek women are still well organized and active. They participate in activities and studies suggested by the Board of Women's Work, and often undertake projects that are entirely their own.

An interesting part of this church is its cemetery. One grave has no name or date. Tradition has it that a stranger passing through the community was thrown from his horse against a tree and killed, and was the first person to be buried at Steele Creek. The first marked grave is dated 1763. The earliest markers simply carry

name and date of birth and death, while later tombs carry long, detailed accounts of the life of the deceased. Here are buried at least a score of Revolutionary War soldiers and the majority of the 240 from this section who entered the Confederate Army.

Now, as always, the church is the center of community life. It stands—as it has stood for nearly 200 years—to remind the people of Steele Creek of the "better way of life."

—B. J. AND FRANCES D. BROWN

Historic Churches of the South

"THE COMMONWEALTH of Kentucky was scarcely four years old when a few citizens of Lexington, the largest settlement in the frontier state, organized the Episcopal Society. It has been 156 years since that meeting took place in a small wooden house on the site of the present building of Christ Church. Before that time, and for ten years thereafter, the activities of Episcopalians in the state appear to have been feeble and unorganized. But as the years went by the Episcopal Society became a strong congregation; many of its members assumed leadership in civic, educational and welfare organizations in the community.

"For several years before the Episcopal Society was founded, members of that group probably held services on the farm of Captain David Sheley on Russell's Road, approximately four miles from Lexington. Aside from these services, history records but one instance of Episcopal worship in this 'western' wilderness.

"There were few Episcopalians among those pioneers who fought their way across the Appalachian mountains,"* to stand at last on "the dark and bloody ground." But when the Revolutionary War was over and the Protestant Episcopal Church was established in 1789, concern was shown for those members in that remote and inaccessible wilderness beyond the mountains. There was an immediate attempt to send missionaries into the new country to assist in planting and spreading religion and learning.

Several clergymen were sent out, but not until the Reverend James Moore settled permanently in Lexington was it practicable to organize the scattered Episcopalians and establish a parish. This

One of the most famous communicants of Lexington's Christ Church was the statesman, Henry Clay, who was baptized there at the age of seventy.

energetic and scholarly man, dividing his time between the newly formed Transylvania Seminary (now a college) and the budding parish, accomplished much in the realms of religion and higher education.

James Lane Allen, in his story "Flute and Violin," describes this first Episcopal minister who permanently located in Kentucky:

"He beat the canebrakes and scoured the buffalo trails for his Virginia Episcopalians, huddled them into a dilapidated little frame house on the site of the present building, and there fired so deadly a volley of sermons at the sinners free of charge that they all became living Christians. Indeed, he fired so long and so well that, several years later—under favor of Heaven and through the success of a lottery—there was built and furnished a small brick church, over which he was regularly called to officiate twice a month, at a salary of two hundred dollars a year."

From that small beginning on a plot of ground above the creek which flowed through the center of the town, Christ Church has grown and prospered, along with the community and the state. The catalog of men and women who figured importantly in the church history between 1796 and 1952 would take more space than allotted here, but the story of Christ Church would not be complete without the mention of at least a few of them.

In 1819, a former rector of Christ Church, Mr. Ward, held the first Episcopal services west of the Mississippi River and organized Christ Church in St. Louis, "the Mother Parish of the West."

In 1822 this same clergyman returned to Lexington and established a coeducational academy in the city with several teachers and over a hundred pupils, one of whom later became Mrs. Abraham Lincoln.

The church purchased the Episcopal Burying Ground in 1834 and on it built a keeper's house which is still one of the finest examples of modified Gothic architecture in America.

The third and present brick church structure was erected on the same site in 1847; and in that same year Henry Clay was baptized, at the age of seventy, having been a pew holder and contributor to the parish for many years. His original home, before Ashland was built, was diagonally across from the church building.

In 1840, Bishop Smith, the first diocesan and a rector of Christ Church, was chosen State Superintendent of Public Instruction. He served the interest of education in Kentucky with the same zeal and enthusiasm he had manifested in his church work, and was widely known as a man of wisdom and foresight.

Around 1890, the Woman's Guild of the parish set up an 80-bed infirmary which they ran for a number of years. Later the other  churches pitched in and helped with this worthy enterprise. In 1905, a larger building in a new location became the Good Samaritan Hospital, run by an interdenominational board. In 1924, the Methodist Church took over full responsibility for it, and today it is one of the two fine modern hospitals in the city.

The members of Christ Church laid the foundation of many other services of religion to the community—from the Baby Milk Supply, the Family Welfare Council and the Council for Social Planning to the Macalester Home for widows and children.

Christ Church parish today is still following in the path set up by its forefathers and continues to furnish leadership for all good enterprises in the community. It has over 1,300 communicants and 1,800 baptized members, one of the finest educational plants in the South, an outstanding organist and choir, and a beautiful chapel and cloister garth in the heart of the city.

—JAMES W. KENNEDY

Christ Church, 1796-1946, a Brief History of its One Hundred and Fifty Years in the Service of Christ, by Elizabeth King Smith and Mary LeGrand Didlake, with the cooperation of Mrs. Hammond Dugan, Margaret King, Joseph C. Graves, and Jerome Thomas, (Whittlet and Shepperson, Richmond, Virginia.)

BETH ELOHIM

*Historic
Churches
of the
South*

CHARLESTON,
SOUTH CAROLINA

*The Cradle
of Reform Judaism
in America*

THE STORY of Charleston's Beth Elohim synagogue reads like something from that age-conscious city's Chamber of Commerce folders: fourth oldest Jewish congregation still in existence in the United States, second oldest synagogue in the United States and the oldest in continuous use, first Reform congregation in the United States.

The history of Jews in the Province of Carolina goes back to 1695, when the Royal Governor, in noting his experience with some Spanish-speaking Floridian Indians he had captured, wrote, "I had a Jew for an interpreter."

The records of two years later list four Jews who were granted citizenship in Charles Town under laws influenced by the friend of the Lords Proprietors, John Locke. (It was not until forty-three years later that the British Parliament authorized the naturalization of Jews everywhere in the colonies.)

Jews were always allowed to worship freely in the Province of Carolina—although the law gave this right to Protestants only—and they could own land and slaves, a right denied them in neighboring Georgia after 1741. As a result of this liberal policy, there was a steady increase in Carolina's Jewish population.

It is reasonable to assume that the Jews of early Charles Town met informally for religious services, though the first official organization of a Jewish group—the beginning of Beth Elohim—dates from the autumn of 1749, at the conclusion of the Jewish New Year, 5510. The only other Jewish congregation in the South at this time was in Savannah.

Beth Elohim is the United States' oldest synagogue in continuous use.

Even before the congregation passed its first half-century mark, the names of several notable men appeared on its rolls. One was Moses Lindo, who made an important contribution to the prosperity of the colony—in which indigo ranked with rice as an export crop—with his work in grading and attempting to standardize indigo exports to England. Moses Lindo had arrived from London, where he had been a leading indigo merchant, in 1762. Six years later he was made Surveyor and Inspector General of Indigo in South Carolina—a position he held until his death just before the Revolution.

Another notable member of the congregation was Joseph Levy, who was commissioned a lieutenant at the time of the Cherokee War of 1760, and was probably the first Jewish officer in America.

115 ...

During the Revolution, more than twenty-five men from the Beth Elohim congregation enlisted in one company of the Militia. Among them was the young Revolutionary hero, Francis Salvador, who came to South Carolina in 1773 and established himself as a planter. The following year he was elected a member of the Provincial Congress of South Carolina—the first Jew to be elected to an important political office in the United States. He was a friend to the influential men of his state whose love of freedom made them sympathetic to the growing spirit of revolution. On August 1, 1776, on an expedition against Indians and Tories near his plantation lands, Salvador was wounded and scalped. He died on the battlefield, with fierce fighting going on around him—the first Jew to give his life for American independence.

The South Carolina Constitution of 1790 provided religious freedom, the right to vote and the right to hold office for all white men—privileges not extended to Jews in England until 1858.

Sharing the post-Revolutionary prosperity which permeated all Charleston—which had by that time changed the spelling of its name—the congregation of Beth Elohim in 1790 numbered fifty-three families, or more than four hundred persons. This was approximately five percent of the white population of what was then the fourth largest city in the United States. A decade later Charleston was to have the largest Jewish population in the country—five hundred, as compared with New York's four hundred.

On September 19, 1794, after four temporary locations, this prosperous congregation consecrated a handsome new synagogue on the site of the present one. Governor Moultrie and civil and military officers attended the ceremonies, along with "a numerous concourse of ladies and gentlemen."

Thirty years later the first signs of the Reform movement, which had begun among Jews in Germany about 1810, began to make their appearance in this congregation that was to lead the Reform movement in the United States. A group of members of Beth

Elohim organized the Reformed Society of Israelites in 1824, the first movement of Reform Judaism in America. This group disbanded in 1883, but destruction paradoxically brought about its revival several years later. The old synagogue burned in 1838, and by 1840 the congregation was preparing to move into its imposing new house of worship (the present one). The petitioners for Reform won a strenuous argument to have an organ placed in the new building. This was the first organ in a synagogue in the United States, and with this step Beth Elohim officially became a Reform congregation.

As distinct from Orthodoxy, Reform Judaism permits the use of instrumental music and allows men and women to sit together; services are comparatively short (about an hour in length) and are conducted in English, and men are not required to wear hats. The Reform movement has spread—particularly among the older Jewish groups in the South—until it accounts for approximately a third of the Jewish congregations in the country.

During the War Between the States, some 180 members of Beth Elohim served with Confederate troops. Judah P. Benjamin, who was later to become Secretary of State of the Confederate Cabinet, was associated in his childhood with Beth Elohim, where his father was a member.

Numbered among the present congregation of some two hundred members are descendants of five or six of Beth Elohim's first families who are buried in the synagogue's cemetery. This cemetery dates back to 1762 and is the largest pre-Revolutionary Jewish cemetery in the United States.

The Hebrew Benevolent Society, the oldest in the country, was founded in 1784, antedating by three decades the Ladies Benevolent Society of Charleston.

The Jewish Sunday school which was begun by the Beth Elohim congregation in 1838 is the second oldest in the United States. (It was founded only a few months after one in Philadelphia.)

The progressive and prosperous congregation of Beth Elohim last year erected the Bicentennial Tabernacle, a handsome activities and Sunday school building. Surrounding their property, which is located near the center of the city, is a graceful iron fence which dates back to the building of the first synagogue there in 1794. The present synagogue, a fine example of Greek Revival architecture, has been for over a century a source of pride to Charleston.

—ELISE PINCKNEY

Historic Churches of the South

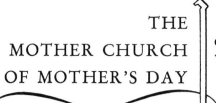

THE MOTHER CHURCH OF MOTHER'S DAY

GRAFTON, WEST VIRGINIA

WORSHIPPERS entering Andrews Methodist Church in Grafton, West Virginia, find a plaque which bears the simple inscription, "The Mother Church of Mother's Day." Inside, on the wall at either side of the pulpit, they see old-fashioned oval portraits of two women—Mrs. Anna Reeves Jarvis, Virginia-born daughter of a Methodist circuit rider, and her daughter, Anna Jarvis.

At one time both of these women were devoted members of the Andrews congregation and teachers in the Sunday school. Mrs. Jarvis began her teaching during the War Between the States. Troubled by the bitterness of the war's aftermath, she stressed tolerance, understanding and friendliness in her classes, and eventually she organized an annual one-day meeting, "Mother's Friendship Day," devoted to neighborliness among mothers. Pleased by the success of these meetings, she expressed the hope that the day might be observed nationally.

After her death, her daughter Anna devoted her time and her fortune to gaining national acceptance of a day dedicated to mothers.

In 1908, Miss Jarvis asked Andrews Church to dedicate a Sunday service to her mother. The service was planned and on May 8, 1908, the pastor, Dr. H. C. Howard, preached from the text, "Son, behold thy mother. Mother, behold thy son." Miss Jarvis provided 500 carnations to decorate the church because to her this flower typified the beauty and fidelity of mother love.

Since that time there has been a Mother's Day service in the

The first Mother's Day service was held in Andrews Methodist Church.

Andrews Church in Grafton on the second Sunday in every May. It was appropriate that on May 8, 1910, the governor of West Virginia issued the first official Mother's Day proclamation. The governors of Texas and Oklahoma issued similar proclamations in 1912, and in 1914 a resolution for the national observance of Mother's Day was introduced in Congress. President Wilson approved it on May 8, 1914. Anna Jarvis' memorial to her mother has grown into an institution cherished by all of us.

Behind the pulpit hang portraits of Mrs. Jarvis and her devoted daughter Anna, who conceived the idea of a national observance of Mother's Day.

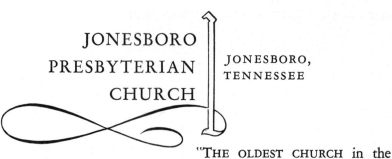

JONESBORO PRESBYTERIAN CHURCH

Historic Churches of the South

"THE OLDEST CHURCH in the oldest town in Tennessee" is the present-day distinction claimed by the Presbyterian Church in Jonesboro, a small town in the northeastern part of the state. And that's pretty old. Although it was not the first one on the early Tennessee frontier, the church does antedate the State of Tennessee itself, which was not admitted to the Union until 1796.

The church was organized in about 1790 by the Reverend Samuel Doak and the Reverend Hezekiah Balch, graduates of Princeton Theological Seminary who had made their way westward over the mountains a few years earlier. They called their new church Hebron, a name retained by the congregation for the next 50 years. Twenty people made up the original membership, but that was a goodly number in proportion to the size of Jonesboro, which in those days was a sparsely populated frontier community.

The town itself was planned and laid out in 1779 as the county seat of North Carolina's Washington County, a huge tract which embraced all of what is now Tennessee.

Hebron Church's first meeting house was a log cabin located on a site four miles east of the new town. The second was a school house, Martin Academy, built in 1816. The upper story of this building housed the academy and the lower floor was used as a place of worship. Later, as the congregation grew, it was often necessary to adjourn to a nearby grove to accommodate the crowds.

The congregation occupied its third building in 1831, though ... 122 this structure was not actually completed until 1836, and even

Jonesboro Presbyterian Church antedates the State of Tennessee itself.

then it had no tower; the bell was hung from a wooden frame which stood at one end of the church. A few years later, when the question of a more suitable bell tower was raised, the congregation decided to erect an entirely new building. And so a fourth house of worship, the one in use today, was built. It was completed in 1850 and dedicated on August 16 of that year. The entire cost of the building *and* its furnishings was $6,420.27.

Built in the Greek Revival style, it rests on a high basement with a paneled entrance. Above the simple pediment rises a steeple, which originally had pinnacles on the four corners of the first stage. The hand-made bricks and shutters, the wide floor boards and the quaint hardware attest to the age of the building. The doors of the pews have been removed, leaving only the hinge notches, but the original pew numbers remain to this day. The altar is a replica of one in a northern church of like faith. The raised pulpit is reached by a stairway on either side. The baptismal font, Communion service and offering plates date from 1860. The old slave gallery is now used as a choir loft.

The church divided in 1868, but the resulting dispute over the property was amicably settled a few years later by an arrangement which provided for joint ownership and occupancy of the building by the two divisions. Joint ownership and occupancy by the two branches, U. S. and U. S. A., continued until 1882 when the northern, or U. S. A., branch relinquished its claim and built the Second Presbyterian Church a block away. Years later, in 1926, union of the two groups was sanctioned by both governing presbyteries, but union of the local congregations was not effected until 1943.

When the merger was finally accomplished, the two congregations set about restoring the old church building. The task was completed and the rededication service held in 1944 under the direction of the Reverend Doctor C. L. Shelby.

The present membership of the church is around 250, and plans call for a $15,000 addition to the building to house a chapel and new nursery, kindergarten, primary and junior classrooms. While proudly conscious of its history and heritage, Jonesboro Presbyterian Church is equally concerned with meeting the present and future needs of the community it has served so long and admirably.

—VIRGINIA WILLIAMS